Beyond the Golden Rule

A Jewish Perspective on Dialogue and Diversity

Beyond the Golden Rule

A Jewish Perspective on Dialogue and Diversity

David A. Kunin

Gaon Books
www.gaonbooks.com

Beyond the Golden Rule: a Jewish Perspective on Dialogue and Diversity
Copyright (c) 2015. David A. Kunin. All rights reserved. This publication is in copyright. Subject to statutory exception and to the provisions of relevant collective licensing agreements, no reproduction of any part may be made without the written permission of Gaon Books, except for brief quotations included in analytical articles, chapters, and reviews.

For permissions, group pricing, and other information contact Gaon Books, P.O. Box 23924, Santa Fe, NM 87502 or write gaonbooks@gmail.com.

Manufactured in the United States of America.
The paper used in this publication is acid free and meets all ANSI (American National Standards for Information Sciences) standards for archival quality paper. All wood product components used in this book are Sustainable Forest Initiative (SFI) certified.

Library of Congress Cataloging-in-Publication Data

Kunin, David A., 1961- author.
 Beyond the golden rule: a Jewish perspective on dialogue and diversity / David A. Kunin. — 1st edition.
     pages cm
 Includes bibliographical references and index.
 ISBN 978-1-935604-71-6 (pbk. : alk. paper) — ISBN 978-1-935604-72-3 (ebook)
 1. Golden rule—Comparative studies. I. Title.
 BL85.K86 2014
 201'.5—dc23
                    2014041214

Contents

	Acknowledgements	7
	Introduction	9
I	The World's Parliament of Religions	15
II	The Golden Rule Narrative	33
III	The Dark Side of the Golden Rule	41
IV	There is an Even Greater Principle	51
V	A New Dialectic	61
VI	Moving Away From Essential Messages	75
VII	Learning to Dialogue for Difference	87
VIII	Narratives of Prayer	101
IX	Moving from Tolerance to Appreciation	109
X	Challenging My Own Tradition	121
XI	The Challenge of Universality	139
XII	Journeys: A Tentative Theology	147
	About the Author	160
	Bibliography	161
	Index	169

Acknowledgements

This book is the product of research, writing and discussion of over twenty-five years, beginning when I was a student at the Jewish Theological Seminary of America. The Seminary was and is the central teaching institution of Conservative Judaism. Its instructors focused on a modern and scholarly understanding of the Jewish traditions. Professors as diverse as Joel Roth, Neil Gillman and Judith Hauptman enabled me to see Judaism as a multivalenced tradition, built of many voices, and enshrining the possibility of a multiplicity of "right" answers. The Seminary also provided my first experiences of interfaith dialogue, as I met and interacted with students from seminaries of other faiths on an intellectual and spiritual level.

I also owe a debt of gratitude to my many colleagues who worked with me in interfaith organizations across the globe, most especially as part of the Southern Tier Interfaith Coalition (Elmira, NY), and the Edmonton Interfaith Center for Education and Action, (Edmonton, Alberta). Community work helped to crystalize my understanding that appreciation of difference should be a primary goal of both formal and informal interfaith dialogue. One of the implicit goals of the Edmonton Interfaith Centre was to allow each religion to speak in its own voice. This helped me to refocus my understanding of the possibilities of interfaith prayer, and education. The Centre's lunch and learn program was also an important venue where my ideas could be shared, discussed and critiqued.

I am particularly indebted to my colleagues and teachers at the University of Alberta. Professors Andrew Gow and Francis Landy have been good friends, teachers and colleagues. My colleagues in the University Chaplaincy – especially Rick Van Manen, Denise Davis-Taylor, Richard Reimer and Audrey Brooks – have also helped me to understand their diverse religious traditions, and I doubt that this book would have reached the level it has without our soul searching discussions on faith, authority and post-modernism. David Goa, director of the University's Chester Ronning Centre, also provided a venue for detailed presentation and discussion of my work.

I am also particularly grateful to Ron Duncan Hart and the staff at Gaon Books for their work in preparing this volume for publication, and for Ron's willingness to present my work to a wider audience.

Finally I would like to thank my family for their support and help in the creation of this volume. My brother Seth has always been my partner in crime. Together, we have discussed and parsed out all of the ideas that have become central to my understanding of both the Jewish tradition and multi-faith interaction. My mother Carolyn also provided essential critique of my work, and has edited every iteration of this book. This book would not have been possible without the intelligent support of my wife Shelley. She was a supportive reader, as well as a constant goad for me to read, think and write.

Introduction

IN 1893, AT THE DAWN OF INTERRELIGIOUS DISCOURSE, multi-ethnic society was more of an ideal than an actuality. Western nations were largely characterized by ecumenical rather then interreligious diversity, and were, nearly, uniformly Christian, with other religions largely relegated to the east. The world was large, and to a great degree disconnected. Over the last hundred years much has changed. Distances have been mitigated by improvements in transportation, and nearly instantaneous communication; while countries like the United States, Australia and Canada have grown increasingly diverse ethnically and religiously. Isolation is also now impossible, as events such as those in the Middle East or Asia have ripple effects across the globe. Adherents of many different religions now live in close proximity, which has the potential to exacerbate conflict. All of these changes and the move to globalization are an impetus for interreligious (and cultural) discourse. We need to understand and accept each other if humanity is going to flourish and even survive in the years to come.

I had my first experiences of interreligious communication as a rabbinical student over thirty years ago. At monthly meetings Jewish and Christian seminarians from across New York[1] gathered to learn about each other and to share experiences. I remember being surprised at the commonalities in the studies of the different schools and in the religious experiences of the participants. It seemed a safe environment to share, without the threat of missionizing, conflict or loud argument. I am unsure if it was intentional, but the topics we examined together were always ones that fostered agreement. Discussions, therefore, focused on safe social issues such as poverty and peace, while more challenging issues such as abortion were assiduously avoided. Even topical issues, such as changing gender roles in religious life (during this period Jewish Theological Seminary of America made the internally divisive decision to accept women into rabbinical school) were never discussed. Matters

---

1 The participating seminaries were Hebrew Union College-Jewish Institute of Religion (Reform Jewish), Jewish Theological Seminary of America (Conservative Jewish), General Theological Seminary (Episcopal), Union Theological Seminary (Protestant), and St Joseph's Seminary (Catholic).

of creed and doctrinal differences were therefore also absent from deliberation. Nevertheless, these regular meetings fostered a sense of cooperative effort, and engendered all of us with a feeling of community and commonality of purpose.

Comfort was also created in the numerous interfaith services (usually held around the American Thanksgiving) that I attended as a student and newly ordained rabbi. Everyone was very careful not to tread on any toes. Prayers offered by a variety of Jewish and Christian clergy (with only very rare inclusion of faith leaders from other traditions) were religion-neutral, with very little particularistic content. The common language was English, and the divine referred to as God, or occasionally as father or lord. These services were not about sharing or teaching, but rather focused on the common need to celebrate and give thanks. The theme of social justice and peace was also often a focus of these services. I know that I always came away with a good feeling that common values united all people of faith.

Commonalities were also the focus of interreligious conferences that I attended both in Europe and the United States. Peace and social justice, topics that fostered general agreement, were the dominant themes. The Golden Rule, (do unto others as you would have others do unto you) which was seen as the root of all positive religious messages, was often highlighted as an ethic that united Jews, Muslims and Christians – it was rare at that time, due perhaps to relatively small populations, for Eastern religion to be represented at events. The conferences aimed, and to a great extent for participants succeeded, in creating a united sense of vision and mission for religion in the late twentieth century.

Yet, after several years of interfaith work, I began to realize that I knew as little about Christianity and Islam (not to mention Buddhism, Sikhism and Hinduism) as I had before I began. All I knew was that we shared the Golden Rule and a united vision to end poverty and war. Was this the sum total of religion; are we really all the same, with just a few unimportant particularities, or are the particularities important? Are they in actuality the essences that define us? Did I, for example, really understand Christianity, without having any knowledge of the importance that Jesus and the Trinity play in many Christians' lives and thoughts? I began to wonder if interreligious discussion could and should have an additional aim beyond the focus on similarity.

At that time I didn't realize that continued ignorance of other traditions' particularities often would come to be connected with a corollary, suggesting that particularities of religious traditions were indeed unnecessary in religions of the future. The message was brought home to me in Hans Küng's *Judaism* (Küng, 1992), a monumental study of Jewish history, belief, practice and thought. In essence Küng, a Catholic, suggests that Judaism will truly be a modern religion when it strips away all its particularities of practice, and focuses on its essence as an expression of ethical monotheism. He also posits that Christianity (devoid of the Trinity) and Islam (devoid of its particularities) are similarly expressions of the same ethical monotheism. Together as post-modern religions the three Abrahamic faiths could work together with the shared ethic of the Golden Rule to create a world guided by the values of peace and justice.

To some degree I was shocked that an outsider should have the effrontery to decide the essence of my tradition, but even more I came to feel that he had misunderstood Judaism as a whole. Faith may define (his understanding of) Christianity, but it is *mitzvot* (the multiplicity of commandments), the very particularisms that he derided, that to me define Judaism. Would Judaism still be Judaism if it were recreated in Küng's image? I think not. Reading Küng enabled me to concretize my belief that it was only through the appreciation and understanding of difference that one can come to a true understanding of the other.

Investigation into the dominant narrative of similarity also pointed to other challenges beyond the loss of individuality and misunderstands of the other. It also suggested a potentially colonialist discourse, where a dominant tradition has the potential to impose itself on less powerful faith expressions. Indeed the quest to identify the Golden Rule, as the essential ethic of religion, potentially poses such a threat, as advocates search out diverse "traditions" and identify versions of the rule, no matter their relative importance in target traditions. Küng's examination of Judaism is an example of just such an imposition.

While the search for similarity and commonality has been the focus of many interfaith interactions there are other possible narratives (inclusivity, exclusivity, pluralism, and unity of mission) to build understanding and acceptance. All these, including the narrative of unity of message, have their roots in the first World Parliament of Religions held in 1893, an event which marked the beginning of modern interreligious communication. The presentations at the parliament demonstrate both the strengths and the weakness of these narratives. Indeed, unity was not the dominant narrative of the Parliament, it was only in the following years up to the present, that it, especially with its focus of the Golden Rule, as the essential message common to all religions, became the dominant narrative of interfaith discourse.

It is the aim of this work to reexamine the dominant guiding narrative built on a search for unity, and to suggest, if necessary, an alternative narrative. It suggests that a narrative of unity built on the Golden Rule, is an expression largely of a single tradition, which is then imposed on others. In a test case, it will be shown that while the Golden Rule may be the essential ethic of Christianity, it plays a much lesser role in the Jewish tradition. The "Rule's" usefulness as a guiding ethic, whatever its provenance, will also be examined. It will be suggested, likewise, that it is insufficient for creating a level playing field necessary for the interaction of equals.

This work focuses on a pluralistic narrative, which places value on each religion as it authentically wishes to be seen and understood. While such a presentation will highlight similarities, it will also highlight difference. Unlike the narrative of unity, these distinctions are not dross to be discarded as unnecessary, but rather are equally (or potentially more) important as the similarities in the identification of the essence of the particular religious tradition. This narrative contends that the goal of interreligious interaction is not the creation of something new, nor is it about transformation of other traditions. Rather its goal is the building of bridges of understanding and acceptance between the diverse religions of the world.

While the pluralistic narrative presented here does not look to change the expression of diverse religions of the world, it does suggest a dialectical shift, to enhance the possibility of peaceful coexistence and interaction. Western thought is built on the Hegelian dialectic, which posits a process where a single synthesis or truth can be identified. This dialectic forms the basis of the modernist search for meta-narratives to create understanding of categories such as world religions. Such meta-narratives, perforce, create criteria that tend to impose zones of exclusion, and broad definitions that have the potential to misunderstand or misrepresent the particular.

The new dialectical model, built on Talmudic and Jain traditions, suggests a very different approach. Instead of a single synthesis or truth, it suggests the simultaneous existence of a multiplicity of truths. This dialectic suggests that each truth statement is true in an absolute sense, but that other truth statements, even those that are contradictory, are also equally expressions of truth. Truth is a matter of perspective, and can even change over time based on contingency and context. This dialectic allows for a non-judgmental dialogue, where understanding of the other, rather than conversion or transformation is the goal.

Concepts of dialogue also require some measure of reexamination. Historically dialogues, whether actual (as in the medieval Jewish-Christian dialogues), or idealized (as in Justin Martyr's *Dialogue with Trypho* (Justin, 2003) or Judah Ha-Levi's *Kuzari* (Halevi, 1969)) were built on the intended goal of proving the truth of one tradition over the others, and thus were expressions of power by the dominant, or in literary works the author's, tradition. While explicit dominance, and desire for conversion has largely disappeared, modern dialogues are still built on a desire for transformation. While the expressed hope is that participants will learn of each other, speakers still often attempt to score points, highlighting the truth of their own tradition, with an implicit hope of convincing others or on occasion more benignly to be transformed themselves. Dialogue also poses the danger of imposition, as we understand and interpret the other based on our own categories and definitions.

To avoid these dangers Martin Buber (Buber, 1970) posits a content-less form of dialogue, built on very brief interactions. He suggests that if an encounter is prolonged we immediately begin the process of imposition, where we objectify the other, turning him/her into an "it" rather than a "you." This danger of such objectification cannot be minimized; yet content is an essential aspect of interreligious dialogue. The model of dialogue suggested below, demands a level of increased consciousness, where participants, to the best of their ability, listen without judgment, or the imposition of categories or objectification.

Language and symbols also pose a unique challenge to interfaith interaction, and can cause confusion and misunderstandings. During interaction with leaders of other traditions I quickly realized that a common language divided us. Words like fellowship, stewardship and grace, not to mention rapture, had a very different meaning for committed Christians than for me, though all of us were native English speakers living in close proximity. Symbols are equally open to a multiplicity of interpretations. The swastika, to name only one powerful example, is a symbol of horror for Jews, while it is a benign symbol of reverence and good fortune found on many Buddhist Temples in Japan. Semiotics (which explains how symbols and words can have a simultaneous multiplicity of meaning) can therefore provide an important theoretical adjunct to assist in meaningful interfaith discourse.

While the aims of multi-faith discourse should not include the goal of transformation, this does not preclude transformation as a byproduct of that discourse and as a legitimate internal development of it. Religious traditions, like all aspects of culture, are not static, but are in a constant state of flux, development and reinterpretation necessitated by internal and external stimuli. The world, in many ways, is becoming smaller and smaller, as communication, transportation, and the availability of information (and misinformation) continue to grow. These changes necessitate a response. Those interested in fostering cooperation, and multi-religious discourse may need to examine their own traditions, not to remove particularity, but rather to excise or reinterpret aspects of their own traditions that impede the acceptance of the legitimacy of the other.

Yet, unlike Küng's attempt at imposition of a reinterpreted Judaism, this transformation cannot be an external process, rather it must be an organic process from within. The last sections of the book, therefore, are an internal "insider" examination of the Jewish tradition from the author's particular contingency and context. They represent an attempt to reinterpret aspects of the Jewish tradition, which have the potential to impede interreligious communication. These are also placed within the context of the author's idiosyncratic theological-mythological system. A discourse which is also placed within the context of the author's personal spiritual journey.

Readers will note that much of the critique and material adduced are derived from, or aimed at the Jewish tradition. It is my belief that one speaks most authentically from (and to) ones own context. It is my hope, however, that the ideas examined are generalizable and of interest to a broader context. There is, however, some material derived from other traditions. While the interpretation of this material is my own, I would like to apologize for any misunderstandings or mischaracterizations.

The World's Parliament of Religions

SEPTEMBER 11, 1893 MARKED A NEW BEGINNING IN THE INTERaction between the world's faith groups. For the first time, as a centerpiece of the Columbian Exposition held in Chicago, representatives of ten faiths gathered together in the World's Parliament of Religions to discuss ways to enhance understanding and cooperation and even the possibility of unifying diverse religious traditions. While the parliament has been rightly critiqued as a product of its time, with all the challenges of racism, social evolution and Protestant triumphalism inherent in the Gilded Age values of the late nineteenth century United States, it was still a unique and transforming event. It was the first public forum where the general public had the opportunity to hear adherents of eastern and western religious traditions on a nearly equal footing. It provided a voice for diverse traditions, especially those of the East, which had been heard previously only through the medium of Christian missionaries. It was also the first opportunity for the missionized to openly confront and challenge the legitimacy of the western attempts not only to actively seek converts, but to belittle and demonize their diverse traditions. The speeches delivered at the parliament reflect all these realities, which together shaped the competing and often conflicting narratives implicit to the event. Yet, the parliament is not merely of historical interest. All the diverse narratives that shape interfaith interaction and understanding in the twenty-first century were present and articulated at the first World's Parliament of Religions.

There has been significant scholarly analysis and critique of the parliament leading up to and subsequent to its one-hundredth anniversary in 1993. Some analyses suggests that the parliament was central in the development of the concept of pluralism, despite the underlying ethnocentric narrative of its organizers and many of the speakers (Seager, 1993). Others contend that the parliament, as part of the Columbian Exposition, could not live up to its lofty goals because of the implicit underlying myth of Western and particularly American Protestant superiority (Burris, 2001). There is also significant scholarly interest in parliamentary presentations particularly from various eastern traditions that countered this dominant foundational narrative (Mullick, 1993). Other scholars have focused on the selection of religions that participated in the parliament and indeed in the creation of the notion of the world's "great religions" (Masuzawa, 2005). While the analysis presented here builds on the existing scholarship, it also examines the parliamentary narratives both synchronically and diachronically in order to understand the functioning of these narratives at the time of the parliament, but also within the present multi-faith movement.

The 1893 Columbian Exposition was one of the first great showpieces demonstrating the power and potential of the United States to the rest of the world. Following in the traditions of the great expositions of Europe (and the smaller less successful events held in the United States) to exalt the host nation, it aimed to present the United States as the Christian imperial successor to Greece and Rome, exemplifying the best of the vision, values and beliefs of all three.[2] It was built on a mythic understanding of the United States as a republic based on universal freedom, where humanity came together to establish a land of liberty and justice for all under the benevolent rule of the Christian (Protestant) father God. According to the myth, the United States was destined to bring this unity to a disparate and divided world. The implicit signification of the architecture of many major structures at the exposition emphasized the embrace of this myth.[3] The central arch, for example, was built in the style of a Roman triumphal arch and crowned with Columbus riding the chariot of a heroic emperor. At its centre was a quote from the Gospel of John, "The truth shall make you free" (Seager, 2009: 15).

This mythic vision was, however, a product of self-delusion as there were many American populations who were excluded from its embrace,

---

2   John Burris (2001) examines the role that international expositions played in the creation and strengthening the mythic view of self of the host nations.

3   This mythic view of the United States as the true heir of the great civilizations of antiquity is also implicit in the Greco-Roman and Egyptian architecture found in Washington, D.C. and other cities throughout the country. Interestingly, Canadian nineteenth century architecture also demonstrates signification of an imperial myth, but rather than Greco-Roman, its antecedents are mostly British.

most often because of race, but also because of religion. African Americans and Hispanics (found at that time mostly in the West and Southwest), for example, were essentially effaced from America's presentation of self, and even with a single exception from any employment at the exposition. The few Native Americans included were presented merely as a historical disappearing relic with little or no relevance to modern American life.[4] The fairly recent and quickly growing Mormon Church was also excluded both from the exposition and from the parliament.

Social evolutionary ideology also played a critical role both in the exposition and in the ultimate decisions about inclusion at the parliament. It was also a shaping force for many of the parliament's narratives, some of which are still prevalent today.[5] Since the publication of *The Origin of Species* in 1859, evolutionary theory was in vogue not only as the explanation of diversity in animal life, but also in human culture. However, despite being connected in popular imagination with Darwin, the generally accepted version of evolution in the Gilded Age (and perhaps even unknowingly today) was that of Herbert Spencer (1820-1903) (Burris, 2001: 65). Unlike Darwinian evolutionary theory, Spencer posited a clear beginning and end point – humanity – for evolution. This was attractive to people who found comfort in a homocentric view of the world, seeing themselves as the goal of evolution, rather than as a part of a random development by way of natural selection.[6] This biological theory was extended beyond the hard sciences and was used as an interpretive device for human society. It postulated that just as organisms developed from

---

4   This virtual exclusion was carried over to the World Parliament of Religions in which there were only two African American presentations and no presentations by speakers from any of America's indigenous populations. There were also no presentations from the Hispanic community, or indeed any of the countries of Central or South America.

5   It is not uncommon to find that the presumption that monotheism is the highest (most evolved) form of religion still pertains. See, for example, Arthur Green, (2010: 28). This may also explain why presentations on Hinduism often shy away from the various gods, and stress the ultimate unity of the divine. It is also notable that presentations on Buddhism stress the philosophical aspects of the tradition, and largely ignore the role that bodhisattvas play in many forms of the tradition.

6   An implicit goal in evolution made Spencer's views attractive to liberal Christians (and presumably Jews) as it left a place for God as the source of the plan. This view is still found today (albeit among adherents of more conservative religious traditions) in the debate on intelligent design.

the simple to the complex, with a clear lineal movement culminating in humanity, so too, a clear "scientific" narrative of human culture was delineated with primitive hunter-gatherer societies at the bottom and Western European and American civilization at the top. Indeed, all the signs[7] present at the Columbian Exposition pointed to the mythic idea that the United States was top of the evolutionary tree of nations, a mythic view of self (with some nuance) which still forms a central part of American self-identity.

The placement of various cultures within the exposition highlighted the social evolutionary model, establishing a clear dichotomy between the civilized and the primitive. The so called "advanced" nations (and indeed religions) – the United States, European nations, with the addition of Japan and India – had their displays in the White City, the central portion of the exposition, while the "less advanced" had theirs in the Midway, an area of display and commerce separated from the main exposition. The Midway, in effect, was the implicit social evolutionary tree imprinted on the fair ground.[8] The only European and American representations in the Midway were historical exhibits of the past, such as Irish castles or traditional German village architecture. The main Midway displays were a variety of "villages" from different "primitive nations," where people lived their "regular" lives, performed their ceremonies, everyday activities and even died for the entertainment of exposition patrons (Burris, 2001: 117-122).[9] The cultures in the Midway included Lapps from Iceland, Javanese, Dahomey and Native American peoples. Even some powerful non-Christian nations had their only representation in the Midway. Islamic nations (such as the Ottoman Empire), for example, were located in the Midway, where a Turkish mosque served both Muslim and Jews.

The expositions both in the White City and in the Midway served to reinforce not only social evolutionary views about various nations,

---

7   My understanding of signs, based on semiotic theory is elaborated in Chapter IX.

8   Placement on the Midway was not based directly on a social evolutionary scale. The Midway was primarily a place of commerce not culture; therefore it was a mix of commercial ventures and displays of "primitive" and "semi-civilized" cultures. Burris suggests that there was a definite weighting of cultures, with the European historical displays as the most prestigious, and the "native" villages as the least. (Burris, 2001: 113.)

9   Burris notes that visitors to the exposition were even disappointed that people in the Inuit display refused to wear their fur parkas in a Chicago summer.

but also about religions, placing monotheism, most especially Protestant Christianity at the top of an evolutionary scale with "primitive religions" at the bottom. One contemptuous contemporaneous social commentator former Virginia governor William E. Cameron,[10] describes the hierarchy below Christianity, based on the expositions placed primarily in the Midway, in clear terms.

> [Buddhism] is not a religion, but a crude system of philosophy embodying the worship of idealized types of manhood through idols and symbols. The Chinese have Joss house where their peculiar forms of idolatry are observed. The Zulus, Fijians, and Samoans have weird beliefs, and their ceremonials are such as to strike pity and disgust upon the mind of enlightened beholders. That gross superstition should maintain its existence in the midst of an occasion which shows forth the fullest flower of civilization and Christianity intensifies the repugnance with which one views the mummeries and grosser rites by which these savages travesty the name of worship (137).

Cameron's distinction between "primitive" and "civilized" cultures and nations was largely accepted in the structure utilized by the planners of the World's Parliament of Religions

Like those who planned the Columbian Exposition as a whole, the principal planners of World's Parliament of Religions were also shaped by the myth of manifest destiny of United States of America and the "scientific" social evolutionary views weighing the value of diverse religions of the world. This world view shaped the narrative that they hoped would guide the deliberations of the parliament, culminating in a modernist narrative of unity, which was largely built on the values and beliefs of Protestant Christianity (Seager, 1993: 8). Adherents of ten ancient religions, categorized as "world religions", were invited to participate. These included representatives from Buddhism, Christianity, Confucianism, Hinduism, Islam, Jainism, Judaism, Shintoism, Taoism and Zoroastrianism. So-called "primitive" traditions were not included in the invitation to participate; these religions were presented or represented only by scholars and missionaries as relics of the past, in language not dissimilar to that quoted above. Nor were more modern traditions such as Baha'i, Sikhism or Mormonism included at the parliament.

---

10   Cameron was also the official historian of the Columbian Exposition (National Governors Association, 2012).

Historian, Tomoko Masuzawa, in her insightful examination of the development of the concept of "World Religions" suggests that the list of traditions invited to the parliament was the culmination of a long process on inclusion and exclusion, which had its roots in the seventeenth century (Masuzawa, 2005: esp. 265-274). This process was largely ethnocentric as Western Christian (for the most part Protestant) scholars and theologians developed the concept of religion, largely based on their own tradition. It is notable that the list of the so-called great religions of the world has remained relatively static from the time of the parliament to the present.

Though in the end largely unsuccessful in shaping the overall discourse, the narrative of a unity built on Christian superiority was highlighted throughout the parliament through the use of liturgies with either implicit or even explicit Christian signification. Each session of the parliament was begun with the communal recitation of the Lord's Prayer and often also included the singing of songs from the Protestant hymnal. Handel's "Halleluiah Chorus" was also sung at the opening and closing of the parliament (Neely, 1994: 4). It was also implicitly supported by the overwhelming representation of Protestant speakers over the course of the parliament.

While the organizers aimed for an event guided by a narrative of essential messages leading to unity among religions, in practicality the actual presenters, coming with their own contingencies and contexts, demonstrated the impossibility of achieving such a goal. Speakers from all the included traditions (including Protestant Christians) brought a variety of narratives that were often very different from that of the organizers, pointing more often to pluralism, or exclusivity, rather than inclusivity or unity. The complexity of narrative, which was present at the outset of the interfaith movement, has continued to be central to the discourse into the twenty-first century. All the narratives expressed at the parliament have remained as the central narratives of interfaith interaction.

Indeed, even the two speeches of welcome delivered by parliament organizers Charles Carroll Bonney and John Henry Barrows demonstrate the complexity of the competing narratives brought to the table at the event. Bonney, a layman from the Swedenborgian Church was president of the World's Congress Auxiliary (a series of meetings, congresses and conventions organized in conjunction with the Columbian Exposition). Barrows, a Presbyterian minister, was chair of the Auxiliary's Department of Religion. Bonney's speech of welcome clearly delineates a narrative of unity with only implicit Christian overtones (Bonney, 1993: 17-22).[11] Barrows, on the other hand, while paying respect to all the religions represented at the parliament, strongly celebrates Protestant Christianity and the United States as presenting the message of unity for the world's religions (Burrows, 1993: 23-30).

Within the context of this chapter it is impossible to examine all of the presentations made at the parliament. Instead, several will be examined in detail as emblematic of the narratives that were central both at the parliament and within the context of the modern interfaith movement. Five narratives dominated the event:
- Inclusivity
- Unity built on shared essential messages
- Exclusivity
- Pluralism
- Unity of mission

Of these, two were built on models of the ultimate unity of religion – one a unity built on the foundation of a particular religion, for the most part Protestant Christianity but open to learning from other traditions; the other based on an idealized syncretistic new religion built on the universal essentials of religion and therefore not directly - explicitly - tied to a particular faith expression. Two other narratives focused on presentations of particular religions, one suggesting exclusivity (that there is one true faith, which alone promises salvation) while the other suggested plurality (these included presentations on particular faiths without statements of exclusive truth). A fifth narrative, built on a limited concept of unity of mission (usually concepts of social justice), suggested areas where religions could come together to build a better world.[12]

---

11 Bonney speech recognizes the value of the spiritual search found in all religious traditions. He suggests, however, that unity will be built on a shared religious ethic, and "the good deeds of a religious life". At the end of his speech he calls for the unity of all religions built on an implicitly Christian and Biblical model, suggesting, "the Golden Rule be the basis of this union" (Bonney, 1993: 22).

12 Other narratives such as the search for Christian unity, presented at the parliament, are not included here as they are germane to the ecumenical, but not the interfaith movement. It could be suggested, however, that these implicitly support a narrative of Christian exclusive truth. The same can also be said concerning the numerous presentations justifying and celebrating Christian missionary activity.

Numerous speakers, mainly from various Christian traditions, focused on a narrative of inclusivity, looking to a time when the world's religions would unite under the gentle embrace of a particular tradition. This narrative suggested that while all religions had elements of truth, only one religion, the bearer of ultimate truths, could bring them all together. The views of two parliamentary speakers embracing this narrative, one Christian and one Hindu, will be examined. Each saw their own tradition as being uniquely placed to be the unifying force.

Lyman Abbott a Congregationalist, and popularizer of liberal Christian theology (Seager, 1993: 35-36) focused on religion as an essential characteristic of humanity (Abbott, 1993: 52-61). His speech encompasses elements of process theology and scientific and social evolution. Abbott suggests that unity is the essence of the creator, and that therefore monotheism is the highest form of religion (57). This model appears to be heavily influenced by the Spencerian theory of social evolution. He claims that history is not a mere narration of events, but rather is the expression of the evidence of progress as cultures evolve into higher forms, an evolution intended by humanity's creator (57). He suggests that religious understanding, as part of this evolutionary chain, is progressing from the pagan to the Christian.

Within this model there is a clear valuation of the various religious expressions found in the world. Abbott accepts all of them as being part of the journey of faith, and therefore all have worth and elements of truth which are important. Indeed, he implies that there is much that a Christian can learn from other religions (59). Yet, Christianity, more particularly Protestant Christianity, is clearly the ultimate evolved tradition expressing the truest understanding of God. He states, "We are glad to know what they tell us, but what we are gladdest of all about is that we can tell them what we have found in our search, and that we have found the Christ" (59). For Abbott, no other revelation transcends or even equals that of the New Testament. It therefore provides a truth that all can and should accept. Indeed, he claims that through Christ, Christianity represents not only the truest expression of religion, but also of morality. Jesus' Golden Rule, he states, is "an ideal that transcends all other ideals written by the pen of poet" (60).

Abbott's implied narrative is an excellent example of inclusive unity since all religions are valued and have much to offer when embraced by the unifying truth of Christianity. Yet, perforce, it does not allow for a discourse of equals. Christian truths can be enhanced by those of other religions, but its truths transcend all the rest, and need no confirmation. This narrative is ultimately a triumphalist expression of colonialist power serving as a justification of missionizing activity – perhaps respectful of the religions of the target populations, but ultimately denying their legitimacy. It does not posit a general umbrella to create its goal of religious unity, but rather its umbrella is Christianity, ready and willing to embrace adherents of all the other religious traditions.

The narrative of Christian inclusivity was one of the most dominant at the Parliament. While, for the most part, liberal Protestants propounded it, it also formed part of Catholic presentations. John Gmeiner, for example, also looks to a unity of world religions, built on both Jesus' Golden Rule and the truest expression of faith, "the Holy Catholic Church." (Gmeiner, 1993: 171).[13]

This narrative, however, was not only propounded by Christians at the World Parliament. Vivekananda, founder of the Vedanta movement and one of the most prominent Hindu attendees also brought it forward. He describes Hinduism as the religion most fit to embrace all others, because it is built on the concept of seeing unity in diversity (Vivekananda, 1993: 430). Vivekananda's model is not evolutionary as he values the lasting ancient traditions over newer ones. Yet, while Judaism and Zoroastrianism are seen as equally ancient, he views Hinduism as the most successful, because of its ability to embrace its divergent children, e.g. Jainism and Buddhism (421). Vivekananda's Hinduism values all religious traditions, because all are inspired by God. But he also suggests that there is an essential unity to religion, and that all the contradictions between faiths are merely apparent, and are but contingent and contextual aspects of the same truth (430). Hinduism he implies is the best hope as the unifying tradition because it alone has the power to embrace the beliefs of all the others.[14]

---

[13] Interestingly while Gmeiner also views Christianity as the apogee of religious expression and part of an evolution (or perhaps more accurately a devolution) of faiths, his model is more traditionally religious (based on a model of fall and redemption) not based on either Spencer or Darwin. Instead, he posits a reverse evolution where humanity has the chance through Christianity to return to a pure worship of the one God after having degenerated over the ages (Seager, 1993: 169-170).

[14] While Vivekananda's longer presentation implies that the Hindu model is the most inclusive of world traditions, he also makes clear in other remarks at the Parliament that his unity did not require that a Christian become a Hindu,

Interestingly, at the 100th anniversary Parliament of World Religions, held in Chicago in 1993, this narrative was embraced by a number of non-Christian religious traditions it was however eschewed by Christian presenters (Neely, 1994: 5). Neely, a conservative Christian commentator on the parliament, notes with disappointment that while Muslims, Hindus, Sikhs, Buddhists, Jains and Zoroastrians all claimed inclusive power for their traditions, Christian presenters (perhaps overcompensating for the presentations at the original parliament) focused only on important, but "peripheral" social issues (5).

Bonney's call for the creation of a syncretistic unified religion built on the essentials found in all religions was also expressed in numerous presentations at the parliament. Like the inclusive narrative discussed above this model also looks to the establishment of a single religion for all humanity. It differs however in that it does not explicitly give priority to any particular religion as having greater access to religious truth. Christopore Jabara, an Archimandrite of the Orthodox Church in Syria, presented one interesting and fairly limited use of this narrative. Jabara calls for a unified religion for the Middle East based on a mix of the essential messages of Christianity and Islam (Jabara, 1993: 198-201). Unitarian Thomas Wentworth Higginson and Reform Jewish Rabbi Emil Gustav Hirsch presented two broader versions of this narrative.

Higginson suggests that all religious beliefs are partial, limited and unsatisfying. Therefore, it requires a mix of all of them together to point to anything that comes close to resembling the truth (Higginson, 1993: 70-74). The great religions of the world are described as sects of the same truth, each having found its own outlet allowing them to approach that truth. He therefore rejects inclusive and exclusive narratives suggesting at the end of his presentation that the "broadest religion" is the best hope for the future (74).

Higginson's use of the narratives is influenced, however, by views of social evolution. Despite his claim to the contrary, a close reading of his speech suggests that he does not view all religions as actually having equal access to the truth. While he makes explicit and numerous mentions of Judaism, Christianity, Islam and Buddhism[15] virtually all

or that a Hindu become a Christian. Rather, he suggests that there are truths in every religious tradition. Taken together, these remarks suggest he fits between two of the narratives adduced above (Seager, 1993: 336-337).

15 The Parsee tradition (Zoroastrianism) is also mentioned once (Higginson, 1993: 73).

other religions are ignored (at least by name). This grouping appears, for Higginson, to represent the apogee of the evolutionary chain. Polytheistic religions (which he labels as idolatrous), on the other hand are scornfully described as groupings of "Hideous fiends and equally hideous gods" (72).

Higginson's narrative of unity is built on the belief that essentials of religion can be identified and can be used to unify the diverse religious traditions of the world. He identifies these truths as "Natural Religion" (74), which he ties to the concept of natural law, spontaneous religious truths, which are the common possession of all humanity. Noting that humanity has a longing for truth of the divine, he indicates that that this search is often expressed through human beings who are seen as incarnating that truth in his or her life. He suggests that Buddha and Jesus are prime examples of such humans. Both, he posits, are incarnations of the unifying truth (71, 72). Benevolent involvement in the community is also a central aspect of natural religion, and as diverse traditions involve themselves in it they come closer together in unity (73).

Despite the universalizing and syncretistic sentiments expressed in his presentation, like Bonney, an implicit Western or indeed Christian bias marks Higginson's search for the essentials of religion. His identification of incarnation, the centrality of benevolent action, and indeed his horror of idols be they in Catholic churches or pagan temples, take values central to Protestantism (and perhaps more particularly Unitarianism of the late nineteenth century) and establishes them as the universals found in each human heart and the essence of "natural religion."

Like Higginson, Hirsch also sees religion as inherent in all humanity and that the essential universal truths can be found and utilized to create a syncretistic unified religion to bring the world together (Hirsch, 1993: 220-227). Indeed, he suggests that a person who does not have a religion is abnormal (220). Therefore, the religious search of all humankind is important and can be part of the creation of a universal religion of the future. Hirsch suggests, however, that no existing religion has the answers that meet the needs of the present. Religions like Hinduism and Judaism are limited because they are tied to a specific nation or people. Christianity, Buddhism and Islam are more relevant because they have shed the chains of ethnicity. But even these traditions have only partial truths that do not contain all the elements necessary to create the unified religion of the future (221-222).

Hirsch clearly lays out the elements that he perceives as the essential messages of religion buried in each human, which for him are the new elements of the universal religion. This new uniting tradition perforce will not embrace any particular nation or ethnicity. It will speak in every language, and embrace images from every tradition (222). To encompass this, it will reject enforced credo and theology, as they limit the human ability to perceive the divine. People will be judged by their actions and not by acceptance of a particular creed or belief (224). Indeed, the new religion will be built on the recognition of obligation to the other (225). Views of sin will be transformed; it will no longer be laden with theological baggage and the fear of hell. Instead, it will be viewed as a weakness to be overcome, as together we work to create an "Eden" in this world (224). Prayer also will be transformed in this new unity. It will no longer be a greedy demand for God to fulfill our needs, but rather will be silent and reverential leading to action (226). There is also an implicit monotheism in Hirsch's speech. The divine is always referred to as God or father.

Hirsch's one explicit use of the Jewish tradition is found in his examination of the afterlife. Quoting from the Talmud, he states "One hour spent here in truly good works ... is more precious than all the life to be" (226). While he accepts the notion that there is an afterlife he adduces that in the new world religion it will not be a central focus, rather the new faith will focus on living a life of service to humanity and God in this world (225).

It is notable that while Hirsch calls for recognition of the universality of religion and its essentials, he appears not to be particularly interested in voices beyond his own. His version of a unified religion for the future is idiosyncratic, and indeed very narrowly construed. Bonney and Higginson both implicitly used their own tradition as the model of the narrative of unity; this is even truer of Hirsch. While at the outset he seems to reject Judaism as the source of unifying truths for the future, in essence his entire presentation is built on premises of Judaism, particularly the Reform Jewish movement in the late nineteenth century.

There is indeed a great deal of similarity between Hirsch's presentation at the parliament and the Pittsburgh Platform (1885), a statement of the essential messages of Reform Judaism which was produced at a conference of Reform rabbis (including Hirsch) eight years before the parliament and built on earlier platforms and writings (Plaut, 1965: 33-34). Like Hirsch's parliament speech, the platform embraces the universality of religion, and rejects the concept of a national religion. It also focuses on human responsibility in this world, rejecting concepts such as hell and eternal punishment for sin. Ethical monotheism is also highlighted as the truest conception of the divine.

Other elements central to Hirsch's presentation are also based on his own tradition. Unlike Christianity and some other religions, Judaism places little importance on authoritative creeds and theologies, and much more emphasis on deeds within this world. Judaism rejects the concept of original sin, and instead sees sin as "missing the mark," leaving room for moral improvement. Judaism also gives priority to silent individual meditative prayer. In addition, as noted above, Hirsh's view of the afterlife is drawn explicitly from Jewish sources. Taken together it is clear that Hirsch's essentials, expressed as the building blocks of a universal religion of the future, are all found in and based on central beliefs of his own religious tradition.

The analysis of Higginson and Hirsch demonstrates the difficulty of this uniting narrative. Neither was able to divorce themselves from their own tradition in their search for unity. Therefore, while the narrative purports to respect all faiths, and to embrace the essential messages that are common to all of them; in truth, the selection of essential messages, either consciously or unconsciously, often reflects the essentials of only the religion of the presenter's.

Many speakers, especially the more conservative Catholic and Protestant presenters, expressed the exclusivist narrative that only one particular tradition explicitly was true and all others were at least to some degree false. This narrative also posited a model of religious unity; however, it required that adherents of all other religious traditions leave their own, and convert to the one true faith. Only one non-Christian, Mohammed (Alexander Russell) Webb, an American convert to Islam, also expressed this narrative, stating that every Muslim "believes that ultimately Islam will be the universal faith (Webb, 1993: 270). Similar sentiments were expressed much more strongly by James Cardinal Gibbons in a presentation entitled, "The Needs of Humanity Supplied by the Catholic Religion" (Gibbons, 1993: 155- 163), and by the Protestant Joseph Cook in "Strategic Certainties of Comparative Religion" (Cooke, 1993: 43-51).

Gibbons begins his presentation with a Christocentric view of history, which could also be viewed in social evolutionary terms. He suggests that before the advent of Christ the world was sunk (except for Judea) in a morass of paganism. With the rise of the Catholic Church, which Gibbons suggests is the mother church, humanity was given a "sublime conception of God, but also a rational idea of man and of his relations to his Creator ... Humanity was rescued from the labyrinth of error in which paganism had involved him" (Gibbons, 1993: 156). Gibbons celebrates the universal aspect of the Catholic Church, which unlike ancient national religions, was the source of salvation for all humanity. "All other religious systems prior to the advent of Christ were national like Judaism, or state-religions like paganism" (156). He also highlights the benevolence of the church and the sense of responsibility for all human beings. He concludes his introduction with the following words, "I am not engaged in a search for the truth; for, by the grace of God, I am conscious that I have found it [in the Catholic Church], and instead of hiding this treasure in my own breast, I long to share it with others, especially as I am none the poorer in making others richer" (157).[16] Gibbons sees the goal of the parliament to "prove all things, and to hold that which is good" (157) as an opportunity to create unity by bringing everyone into the one Catholic universal church.

Joseph Cook a Boston evangelical, presented one of the strongest exclusivist narratives at the parliament (Cook, 1993: 43-51). He begins his speech, tendentiously labeling nearly all the non-Christians present (including Muslims, Buddhists, Hindus and Confucians) as infidels, stating that none of these traditions have the power to wash people of sin (47). Indeed, he states that because Christianity has the sole possession of the truth, it provides the only entryway to heaven. This truth is, he suggests, an aspect of natural religion, inherently obvious (when realized) by every human being (48).

When Cook turns to the idea of a universal religion, he posits a narrative that is purely Christian. He suggests "nothing will free us from the necessity of harmonizing our religious faiths" (48). This will not, however, be a harmonization of equals, rather, it shall be a harmonization based on the self-evident truth of Christianity (48). Based on this he adduces two principles of universal religion; surrender to the self-evident truth of science and Scripture, and imitation of the life of Christ (49). The unity he proposes is the exclusive unity of Western, more particularly Protestant, Christianity.

---

16   Gibbons recognizes the benevolent contributions of other Christian Churches, but he suggests that The Catholic Church was first in the field, and the others imitate the actions of the mother church (p. 163). He also implies that the doctrines of other churches are derivative from the Catholic Church which has sole possession of the truth.

There was also a counter narrative to the message of unity, be it inclusive or exclusive, prevalent at the parliament. Speakers from a variety of traditions, non-Christian for the most part,[17] focused on increasing understanding and appreciation of their traditions by a wider audience with no apparent desire to suggest that their tradition was the ultimate truth (even if they believed this). Many of these speakers were from religions little known in the West and had either faced persecution, and/or colonialist proselytization, by western missionaries.[18] The common thread among them is an implicit or even explicit plea for legitimacy and respect. Indeed, an additional goal of many of these presentations was to dispel stereotypes and misconceptions common in the West, and often annunciated at the parliament, even by liberal Christian speakers. This narrative is denominated as pluralist.

Perhaps the strongest presentation of this type was the rebuke addressed to America, the European nations and their missionaries by Hirai Ryuge Kinzo (Kinza Riuge M. Hirai), in a presentation entitled, "The Real Position of Japan toward Christianity" (Hirai, 1993: 397-405). He examines the long period of contact between Western countries and Japan demonstrating the consistent disrespect from the time of first contact to the present. The Christian west, he contends, condemns the entire nation, "as heathen" (397). Moreover, with the opening of Japan by Commodore Perry, unfair and unequal laws had been imposed by Western nations on Japan; excesses, which he ironically suggests were based on the perception that Japan was not "civilized" (401). He thanks the West for its "kindness" in sending missionaries to Japan, suggesting however that the Japanese saw through their hypocrisy. It is impossible, he contends, for them to have any success in Japan, not because Christianity is bad in any way, but rather because the message is not matched by the action of the speakers (or more especially their nations) (402). How, for example, can Japanese people take Christian morality seriously, when the Christian United States shows consistent prejudice towards Japanese people who live in its midst (403).

The fifth narrative is also a narrative of unity, but it is much more limited than those discussed above. Instead of looking to the creation of a single world religion, however it would be constructed, it looks to

17   The few speakers representing a variety of Christian Orthodox churches, for the most part, were included in this category.

18   This complaint was even expressed by Orthodox Christians who resented missionizing by Protestants from the United States and Europe (Tcheraz, 1993: 193)

a unity of purpose on a particular issue of social justice. Most prominent among these are calls for unity to address racism (Williams, 1993: 142-150), anti-Semitism (Berkowitz, 1993: 228-233) and peace (Soyen, 1993: 352-353). Two examples of this narrative will be examined; Shaku Soyen's call for unity to work for peace (Soyen, 1993: 352-353) and Fannie Barrier Williams' call to end racism against African Americans (Williams, 1993: 142-150).

Soyen, a Buddhist, presents a clear message of cooperation based on the creation of a peaceful society. While recognizing the legitimate existence of different and discrete traditions, he suggests that religions can unite in the limited goal of working together to create a climate of peace through encouragement of arbitration instead of war (Soyen, 1993: 352). "We are not born to fight one against another," he states, but rather to "enlighten our wisdom and cultivate our virtues" (352). Peace, as an "essential" of all religions, can lead to a unity of purpose in transformation of the world.

Williams also does not focus on the formation of a world religion, but instead on a more limited goal to end racial intolerance, particularly by American Christians against African Americans. She highlights the negative role that religion – particularly Christianity – played in supporting slavery and intolerance, noting that conversion of the slave to Christianity was used as cynical means of social control, "If Christianity could make the negro docile, domestic, and less independent and fighting savage, let it be preached to that extent and no further" (Williams, 1993: 143). She notes however that it also, to some extent, played a positive role following the Civil War (146). Yet, she also suggests that racism and poverty were still endemic, and that even potentially positive Christian values like the Golden Rule "become in practice the iron rule of race hatred" (149). She concludes with a call for religions for to join together with a shared message "that all souls, of whatever color, shall be included within the blessed circle of its influence" (150).

Each of these five narratives (**inclusivity, unity, exclusivity, pluralism,** and **unity of mission**) in some form or another has remained a central aspect of interfaith interaction. This can be illustrated by a brief description of papers offered at an interfaith symposium, *Opiate of the Masses? Religions in the 21st Century* held in Edmonton in 2010 (Edmonton Interfaith Centre, 2012). A Christian presenter examined the role that the United Church of Canada played in the twentieth century, and adduced from his church teachings social values that could unite religions to work together in the twenty-first; the Jewish presenter talked about the valuable role that religions played in human society, trying to infer the essential contributions of religion, implicitly drawing on his own tradition as his source; the Baha'I presenter suggested that her tradition, containing as it did the essence of all religions, was uniquely placed to unite all the rest as the one true religion; the Wicca presenter called for understanding and asked that people no longer stigmatize her tradition; and a presenter from the Mennonite Christian tradition asked that people from disparate traditions work together to bring peace to the world.

While all five narratives still are central to interfaith interaction, in his comprehensive survey of interfaith organizations, *Inter-Faith Organizations, 1893-1979*, Marcus Braybrooke demonstrates that the two dominant discourses that shape the movement are the search for essential unifying messages and unity of mission to achieve a more limited end, world peace (Braybrooke, 1983: xi). The first narrative, which he labels as the "mystical unity of religion", brings together such disparate organizations as the World Congress of Faith, The Temple of Understanding and the Global Congress of World Religions. The second led to the creation of the National Interfaith Conference on Peace, the World Conference on Religion and Peace, and Religious Workers for Lasting Peace.

These particular narratives may have become the focus of interfaith interaction because they are the least divisive and difficult. It is always safer to focus on similarity and cooperation rather than difference. These narratives also fit best with a modernist meta-narrative that attempts to find broad unity within the various taxonomies of human existence, including religion. They fit with this search as they identify the "essential" or even "mystical" unity of religion. This can even be seen within the limited search for a unity of mission.

These two narratives have continued to shape interfaith conferences around the globe; on an international, national and local level. The 1993 Parliament of World Religions, held in Chicago on the 100th anniversary of the first, focused on a document largely drawn up by Hans Küng, entitled "Towards a Global Ethic: An Initial Declaration" (Küng, 1993). The Declaration embraces both narratives. In its introduction, the document states, "We affirm that a common set of core values is found in the teachings of all religions, and that these form the basis of a global ethic. We affirm that this truth is already known, but yet to be lived in heart and action" (Küng, 1993). The Global Ethic suggests, and subsequent Parliaments addressed cooperation among traditions on social issues as diverse as the environment, peace and aboriginal rights. Local conferences follow a similar model. One recent interfaith meeting, held in Phoenix in 2011, was titled, "Many People, Many Faiths - One Common Principle, THE GOLDEN RULE [emphasis from the conference website]" (Arizona Interfaith Movement, 2012). The conference focused largely on the utilization of this "shared" universal ethic as a means of bringing religious traditions together to facilitate the finding of solutions to social and political problems confronting humanity.

This chapter has suggested that there is a direct continuity between the narratives of the first 1893 World's Parliament of Religions and the discourse of the multi-faith movement of the present. Yet, while all five of its narratives still pertain, only the two dealing with relative degrees of unity dominate the discourse. As has been suggested, however, narratives of unity most often seemed to grant either an implicit or explicit prioritization to one or at best a constellation of traditions. This raises the challenging notion, which requires further investigation, that the current discourse may blind us to the realities of the other as we see and work with other faiths only in terms of our own traditions.

II

The Golden Rule Narrative

The Golden Rule, do unto others as you would have them do unto you, was present at the 1893 World's Parliament of Religions as part of a narrative to create unity through the identification of essential messages among religions. Indeed, Charles Bonney, the convener of the Parliament, stated in the call for the parliament, that the Golden Rule would play a pivotal role in uniting world religions (Seager, 1993: 8). While this idealistic goal had only limited success at the parliament, in subsequent years his vision of its power has been substantially confirmed.

Jeffrey Wattles, in his influential book on the Golden Rule, suggests that it was the most frequently mentioned principle of morality at the parliament (Wattles, 1996: 91).[19] While the veracity of the statement would be difficult to verify, the Golden Rule was indeed frequently invoked. These, however, were made almost entirely by Jews and Christians.[20] In each case when the Golden Rule, was adduced as the building block of religious unity, its connection as the contribution of one or the other of these traditions was also mentioned.[21] Indeed, this is most clearly expressed in the one presentation at the parliament where the rule is connected with non-Christian sources, that of Nobuta Kishimoto a Japanese Christian. He suggests that, "the golden rule is the glory of Christianity, not because it was originated by Christ – this rule was also taught by Buddha and Lao-tse many centuries before – but because Christ alone properly emphasized it by his

---

19 See also (Wattles, 1996) notes 5 and 6, p. 217.

20 The only non-Christian mention of the Golden Rule that Wattles adduces is that of the Confucian, Pung Kwang Yu. Yet Pung Kwang Yu does not mention it as an expression of Confucianism, rather, he includes it in a listing of short maxims from the Christian Bible. He suggests that these short maxims concerning social relations are similar to those of Confucianism, and that his tradition can value them because of their terseness. (Yu, 2010: 429-430).

21 See for example, Seager (1993), *pp.* 60, 64, 96, 166, 214, 232, 381, and 468. In each case a Christian or Jew presents the Golden Rule as the contribution of his religion that can unite disparate traditions.

words and by his life" (Kishimoto, 2010: 1282). It is clear that for attendees at the parliament the Golden Rule was not an expression of a narrative identifying the essential messages of all traditions, rather it was an expression more closely related to the narrative of unity built on the values of one, or in this case two, particular traditions.

The unifying power and the assumption of universality of the Golden Rule, had, however, a long history prior to the World's Parliament of Religions. Many voices stemming from the West have seen the Golden Rule, (also denoted as the ethic of reciprocity) as a foundational ethic of civilization. It was widely known, and communicated in schools, religious institutions and in popular culture long before (and indeed after) the parliament. North American children, no matter their cultural or religious heritage, from their earliest years are still encouraged to live by the rule, and to see it as the ethical basis of their interaction with others. It was and is still perceived as an ethic upon which everyone can agree, a universalizing essential message of religion that can bring together a disparate world.

While there are many cognates of the Golden Rule in ancient and modern traditions, the origin of its universalizing power is found most notably in Christian scriptural formulations, and in subsequent Christian theological and philosophical presentations.[22] The power and centrality of the rule within the western canonical tradition, seeing it as a universal human ethic – a statement of natural law – has played a pivotal role in enabling it to become one of the dominant narratives of interreligious interaction.

Two of three versions of the Golden Rule (all reported as words of Jesus) included in Christian scripture, found in the Gospel of Matthew (7:12, 22:39-40), stress its universal importance as the essence of God's revelation.[23] While the formulations of the rule differ, each text includes an identical conclusion, that it (the Golden Rule) is the entirety of Torah and Prophets. The first formulation, "Therefore all things whatsoever you would that men should do to you, do you even so to them; for this is the law and the prophets." (Matthew 7:12), is included as part of the Sermon on the Mount, a collection of diverse teachings attributed to Jesus. The second, included as a response to a challenge posed by contempo-

---

22   Jewish antecedents and interpretations will be examined in a later chapter.
23   The third formulation of the rule is found in Luke 6:31. This version does not include the universalizing statement included in the versions found in Matthew.

rary Jewish authorities, quotes directly from Hebrew scripture (Leviticus 19:18) "Love the Lord your God [and]…Love thy neighbor as thyself" and concludes with a nearly identical conclusion, "[on these law] hangs all the law and the prophets." (Matthew 22:37-40)[24]

The concluding statement found with both of these texts, that the rule encapsulates the entirety of the law and the prophets, places it as the centre of revelation. The terms "law" and "prophets" are not haphazard or coincidental, rather each, especially taken together, would have had important resonances for Jewish listeners/readers of these words attributed to Jesus. Within the Jewish tradition the Hebrew Bible is made up of three discrete units, with varying weights of authority. The first five books are referred to as the Torah or the Five Books of Moses. These are followed by twenty-one books, beginning with Joshua and concluding with Malachi, which are considered to be works of prophecy, and are called *Nevi'im*, literally the Prophets. The final thirteen books, including such diverse texts as Psalms, Job, Esther and Chronicles, are referred to as *Kithuvim*, or the Writings.[25] Together all these books form the *Tanakh*, or Hebrew Bible.[26] For religious Jews, the earlier books have much greater authority than the later. Thus, the Torah is viewed as the direct revelation to Moses and the Jewish people at Sinai, the books in *Nevi'im* are also considered prophetic, but to a lesser degree than the Torah. The books in *Kethuvim*, on the other hand, while considered to be written under the influence of holy spirit (*ruah hakodesh*), are not considered to be works of direct prophecy. Thus, the statements found in Matthew suggest that the Golden Rule encapsulates the entirety of the Law (Torah) and the Prophets (*Nevi'im*), which the listener would identify as the pivotal sections of the Hebrew Bible.[27]

---

24 The identification of Leviticus 19:18, quoted in Matthew 22:39, as both source and version of the Golden rule is supported in the Christian tradition by Augustine and Thomas Aquinas (Wattles 1996: 72, 73 and n. 19 (chap. 6)).

25 The order of books in the Hebrew and Christian Bibles is not identical. Many of the books included in Writings are placed earlier in Christian Bibles.

26 Tanakh is an acronym of the three parts of the Bible: T(orah), N(evi'im) and Kh(tuvim).

27 The centrality of the first two sections of the Hebrew Bible was (and is) reinforced weekly as part of the synagogue ritual. Readings from Torah and *Nevi'im* are the highlight of every Sabbath and Festival morning service. The books included in *Kethuvim*, on the other hand play a decidedly less liturgical role. Only five (*The Song of Songs, Ruth, Lamentations, Ecclesiastes,* and *Esther*) are read in their entirety during the course of the year.

It would thus be the essence and central message of God's revelation to humanity.[28]

Interestingly, the second of these texts has a direct parallel in rabbinic literature. Jesus's quotation from Leviticus, restating the centrality of the Golden Rule is included as a response to a question, "Which is the great commandment of the law?" posed by a Pharisee, purportedly as a "temptation" to Jesus (Matthew 22:34-36). While the question is problematized in Christian scripture, in actuality it was viewed as legitimate in a relatively contemporaneous rabbinic text (Sifra 89b). In this text two well-known rabbis discuss the exact same issue, namely identifying the great commandment or principle (*klal gadol*) of the Torah.[29] Similar to Jesus, one rabbi (Akiba) identifies Leviticus 19:18 ("Love your neighbor…"), while the other (Ben Azzai) suggest that Genesis 5:1 ("This is the book of the generations of Adam") is the essential principle. The major difference between these texts is perhaps the authority of the answer. The New Testament text presents the answer as unchallenged and in essence gives it the authority of revelation as it is spoken by Jesus. The Midrash, on the other hand, presents two very different human answers, without any indication, which should be viewed as correct.

The universal nature of the Golden Rule, was even more strongly established in Patristic and later Christian writing, where it was seen as a formulation of natural law. Such laws are considered not to be of human origin, but rather to be inherent in nature, and therefore universal. Natural law was an important concept within both the ancient philosophical and Christian theological systems. There was, however, an important distinction between the two. For the philosopher, natural law was the expression of the instincts and emotions common to humanity and the lower animals, while to the Christian theologian it was an expression of divine law written on the soul of each human being. Despite the distinction both systems view natural law as universal. Justin Martyr, for example, claims that God "sets before every race of mankind that which is always and universally just" (Justin Martyr, 1885: 658). He suggests that natural justice or righteousness is exemplified by the Golden Rule (658). Augustine also viewed the Golden Rule, as natural law, written on the conscience of every human

---

28   Both ancient (and many modern) Christians and Jews, listening to this text, would hear an inter-textual reference to Isaiah 2:2-4, which suggests that in messianic times the Torah will be the universal message accepted by humankind.

29   See Chapter IV for a more detailed discussion.

being (Wattles: 70). This Augustinian view, was carried forward into the Middle Ages, was especially influential for Aquinas. He also directly equated the Golden Rule, with Leviticus 19, stating that it was the explanation of the means of observing the biblical commandment to "love one's neighbor" (Aquinas: 2005).

While the universalistic understanding of the Golden Rule, as an aspect of natural law (whether written in the human soul by God or a natural process) remained a central underpinning of its continued religious and philosophical importance, there were several early modern thinkers who challenged both the validity of the concept of natural law, and the centrality of the Golden Rule. Bishop William of St. David's, on one hand, in his *The Comprehensive Rule of Righteousness, Do as You Would Be Done By* (published in 1679), the first book to identify the Golden Rule by name, stresses that it is a "law of nature" universal to all humankind. Indeed, the author suggests that all virtues can be derived from the Golden Rule (79).

On the other hand, while religious authorities may have accepted the rule in an uncritical manner, philosophers and thinkers from John Locke to Bertrand Russell have critiqued it, since the Age of Enlightenment. John Locke, for example, rejects the existence of laws set in each human by God or by nature. He suggests that there are no innate ideas implanted in each mind, rather the mind begins as a blank slate, and is shaped by its contextuality and contingency. Every ethic, including the Golden Rule, is subject to empirical questioning and requires proof (Locke, 1959: 68). Others noted the inability of the rule to deal with people stemming from diverse backgrounds, with differing needs and desires. George Bernard Shaw noting this critique suggested a different challenging formulation, "Do not do unto others as you would that they should do unto you, their tastes may not be the same." He also suggested, "The golden rule is there are no golden rules" (Shaw: 1999).[30]

Kant also challenges the inability of the rule to be sufficiently universal so as to be sensitive to all situations. While differentiating between the Golden Rule and the categorical imperative in *Groundwork for the Metaphysics of Morals*, he notes:

---

30   Shaw also paraphrases the text from Leviticus, "Do not love your neighbor as yourself. If you are on good terms with yourself it is an impertinence, if on bad, an injury" (Shaw, 1999)

It does not contain the principle of duties to oneself, nor of the duties of benevolence to others (for many a one would gladly consent that others should not benefit him, provided only that he might be excused from showing benevolence to them), nor finally that of duties of strict obligation to one another, for on this principle the criminal might argue against the judge who punishes him, and so on" (Kant, 2004: 10).

Not only does the Golden Rule ignore idiosyncratic needs, he also suggests that it does not sufficiently provide for an obligation of benevolence to the "other." Kant also points to a fallacy that he claims is built into the biblical command to "love ones neighbor," suggesting that true love cannot be compelled (10).

Some twentieth century philosophers and religious thinkers have returned to an understanding of the Golden Rule, as a universal statement of ethics, reconnecting it with the concept of natural law. Henry Sedgwick (1962: 379-80) and Marcus Singer (1963: 293-314) both suggest, for example, that its truth is self evident, and that it is the most effective instrument of moral education. Hans Reiner returned to medieval and early modern philosophical theories, seeing the Golden Rule as natural law, which therefore transcended particularistic human conditions (Wattles1996: 147).[31]

Despite philosophical challenges to the universality of the Golden Rule by some philosophers, by the nineteenth century many, especially in the United States, perceived it as the essence of religion and ethics. Diplomats saw it as the underlying value of American relations with other nations (93).[32] Businessmen saw it as the means of running a successful, yet Christian/humane business (97-103). Golden Rule brotherhoods were founded to memorialize it and spread its message (93-95). Jeffrey Wattles suggests that these brotherhoods, though not primarily religious in nature, saw the Golden Rule as having the potential to "bring about

---

31   The concept of natural law, in connection with the Golden Rule and other "essential messages" that unify religions is implied in the goals set forth at the second Parliament of World Religions. It was claimed in "Towards a Global Ethic" that there were core values, most centrally the Golden Rule, that were found in the teachings of all religions, and that these truths were already known in all hearts (Küng).

32   John Hay, Secretary of State under Presidents McKinley and Roosevelt, identified the Golden Rule, and the Monroe doctrine as the two pillars of American diplomacy.

the ecumenical unification of Christianity, harmony between Judaism and Christianity, and eventually the unity of humankind" (94). Religious leaders also saw it as a means of achieving unity between the diverse denominations of Christianity, and ultimately of world religions. Due to these idealistic utopian hopes, The Golden Rule, came to play, as has been noted, a central role the World's Parliament of Religions, held as part of the Columbian Exposition in Chicago in 1893.

The Golden Rule also played a central role in interfaith action following the parliament, especially in the late twentieth and early twenty-first centuries. While speakers at the parliament focused almost entirely on Christian and Jewish origins, and indeed ownership of the rule, as noted earlier tangential connections with other traditions, notably Buddhism and Taoism, were made during the presentation by Nobuto Kishimoto. This may have helped to reify the idea that the Golden Rule was indeed an aspect of natural law, and was the religious message that was common to all humanity. This realization led to the discovery that many religious traditions across the globe embraced ethical maxims that were related in some way to the Golden Rule. While the traditions were not identical, some were positive and some were negative, the similarities were deemed sufficient to support a claim that the Golden Rule was the elusive essential message of religion and a global ethic for the twenty-first century.

The Second Parliament of World Religions held on the hundredth anniversary of the first embraced this message. The Parliament issued *Towards a Global Ethic: an Initial Declaration*, in which the Golden Rule plays a central role. This statement commits its 143 signatories from many of the world's religious traditions to work to solve the critical challenges facing humanity using an ethic largely built upon the Golden Rule. Indeed the rule is paraphrased as the opening to the central paragraph of the declaration, which introduces all of the commitments to humanity and the world, which the signatories affirm (Küng).

The joint religious statement was pivotal in the creation of a Golden Rule movement dedicated to the fulfillment its challenging agenda through the implementation of the rule. Conferences, websites, posters, TV infomercials and even license plates embrace the unifying and almost salvific power of the Golden Rule.[33] Identification, therefore, of the

---

33 Posters and other materials, which support the narrative that the "Golden Rule is, at least one of, the essential messages of religion can be found

rule in diverse traditions has become a central goal of much of the interfaith discourse since it is seen as the similarity, the "essential message," that will override all difference, and solve all conflicts. Thus, for example, as noted above, a recent interfaith meeting was entitled, "Many People, Many Faiths - One Common Principle, THE GOLDEN RULE [emphasis from the conference website]."[34] Indeed, April 5th, with the support of the United Nations, was declared Golden Rule Day.[35] Advocates hope that the UN will grant this as an official designation.

The identification of the Golden Rule as the essential uniting message of religion has become one of the dominant narratives shaping interfaith discourse, as foretold by Bonney in the invitation sent out for the first World's Parliament. Since 1893 it has moved from being the spiritual message and gift to humanity of only two religions, to being perceived the ubiquitous found in all faiths. Indeed, following Bonney's lead, it has been suggested that the Golden Rule should be "uniting ethic" which brings together all humanity's diverse traditions (Wattles, 1996: 165-189).

---

on the websites of nearly every major interfaith organization. The narrative was found, were found, for example on the URI (United Religions Initiative), NAIN (North American Interfaith Network), WCF (World Congress of Faith), Council for the Parliament of World Religions, Temple of Understanding). It was also found on nearly all of the websites of local interfaith organizations. Indeed, an Internet search identified more than 24 distinct posters (ignoring versions of the same poster in different languages), which attempt to demonstrate the ubiquitous nature of the rule.

34   The theme of annual meeting of NAIN (North American Interfaith Network) held in Phoenix in 2011.

35   Following Ethiopia's lead a number of countries have granted this designation.   Nainblog.wordpress.com/2011/03/28/scarboro-golden-rule-movie-screened-at-united nations/

III

The Dark Side of the Golden Rule

THE GOLDEN RULE PLAYED A CENTRAL ROLE AT THE 1893 World's Parliament of Religions, in Christian and Jewish presentations that embraced both the inclusive and exclusive narratives of interfaith interaction. Since then, as has been examined, it has continued to play an important, even dominant role, in the discourse, specifically with the advocates of inclusivity. It has become the most commonly quoted shared ethic, or essential message that is seen as having the potential of uniting all the religions of the world. Its suggested ubiquity is therefore celebrated at conferences, and in numerous books and websites.

While the rule can play an important role in the arsenal of human ethics, the movement to unite religion under its banner is not without danger. Indeed, for traditions such as Judaism that embrace a formulation of the rule it can be an important ideal, asking adherents to consider the needs and desires of others as we make decisions about how we will treat our fellows. It serves, however, more as a slogan than as a self-sufficient rule that will solve all of humanity's social problems. Such limitations are found in all human attempts at creating overarching principles, yet they are not the greatest danger created by the Golden Rule movement. The claim of Golden Rule activists that it is ubiquitous, can blind people both to the real differences between traditions, and can even paradoxically serve to exclude those traditions that may not share a formulation of the Golden Rule.[36]

Advocates of the Golden Rule believe that it is a universal ethic, which is both the basis of all human relations and a means of creating harmony between diverse peoples and traditions. Yet, a statement as broadly construed as the Golden Rule is open to significant misinterpretation and misuse. Indeed, as noted earlier (p. 33), the challenges posed

---

36 It has also been pointed out that the "Golden Rule as the universal uniting ethic as it fails to address our obligations to the natural world. "The Golden Rule does not address our obligation to the flora and fauna or indeed to the earth itself." (Don Frew, 2011).

by misinterpretation have been the fodder of philosophical and literary debate for the last three hundred years by thinkers as diverse as Locke, Kant and Shaw. These challenges have impelled modern advocates even to suggest new wordings to attempt to solve basic problems of interpretation, which are implied in the traditional formulations. Harry Gensler, for example, suggests the following alternative reading, "Treat others only as you consent to being treated in the same situation" (Gensler, 2012).[37] Despite the changes, however, this formulation is as problematic as the actual versions adduced in diverse traditions. Far from bringing people together, the strict (and indeed loose) interpretations of the Golden Rule pose the danger of complicating interfaith interaction.

While there are many ways that this and other commonly adduced versions of the Golden Rule, can be misused or misinterpreted leading to ethical quandaries, two are most germane, both in their misinterpretations and even in the suggested reinterpretations, to multi-faith relations and understanding. Gensler identifies and attempts to deal with these "misinterpretations" which he labels as the "Literal-Golden Rule Fallacy" and the "Soft-Golden Rule Fallacy"(Gensler, 2012).[38]

Gensler defines the "Literal-Golden Rule Fallacy," as the assumption that everyone has the same likes and dislikes (Gensler, 2012). Thus, he rightly suggests, people take the Golden Rule too literally and determine that everyone should be treated exactly the same, they ignore all needs and differences. He suggests that this misinterpretation needs to be qualified by an imaginative leap where one places him or herself in the shoes of the other person. This, he suggests, would allow for an analysis of the situation enabling a better decision on how the other should be treated. Yet, while the leap of imagination may make this possible, its effectiveness is constrained by the level of knowledge of the other. If, for example, the other person comes from a very different culture or tradition, is it truly possible to have sufficient knowledge to understand what he or she needs or wants? Gensler provides an example of a monkey realizing that a fish needs water to survive. This, however, requires a level of knowledge. If the monkey knows nothing of fish, than this realization may never occur.

---

37 A commonly known alternative, the "Platinum Rule", (Treat others as they would want to be treated,) solves some of the issues implied in the Golden Rule, but is not ubiquitous, nor may it be possible to implement.

38 These two fallacies are identified by Gensler with the suggested reinterpretations.

Within the context of multi-faith relations the danger of making assumptions without sufficient knowledge can lead to misunderstandings and bad feeling. The provision of food, for example, at an interfaith gathering, based on the assumption that sharing food will bring people together, without sufficient knowledge of diverse food taboos found in many traditions can create discomfort and prevent rather than facilitate dialogue. Within a broader context the assumption that the same economic or political system will work everywhere on the globe in exactly the same manner, without sufficient local knowledge, can lead to poverty, economic upheaval and political unrest.

It may be that within the context of multi-cultural and interfaith relations that the challenges rendered to Golden Rule, by this fallacy, even with Gensler's correction, makes it unworkable. The effectiveness of the imaginative leap requires a level of knowledge of the other person that may be impossible to attain. Even if, for example, we know that Gensler's fish requires water, we may not know if it requires fresh or sea water. We may not know the minerals and other sources of food that it requires in that water for survival, and we may not know what predators are present in the body of water.

The imaginative leap would also require the elimination of interpretation. Perforce, as we attain knowledge of other persons or traditions our minds synthesize and systematize that knowledge to fit within own accepted models and modes of thought. This leads to the transformation of the "other" as we highlight aspects that are important to us, but may not be important to them. We may also down play aspects, which he/she may hold to be central. Ultimately, therefore, the leap of imagination defines needs, as we see the other persons, rather than the way they really are.

Stereotyping and the development of broad taxonomies can also lead to a misinterpretation and mistaken assumptions. One may assume that every Jew is kosher, or even is pro-Israel, based on a general knowledge of the Jewish people. I have, for example, been at multi-faith events held at or sponsored by Jewish institutions where Muslim participants feel comfortable eating meat, based on the mistaken assumption that it is kosher.[39]

Broad taxonomies and even positive stereotypes fail to take into consideration the complexities of group dynamics and identity construction. There may be, for example, differences between people of

---

39 These events were sponsored by institutions, which do not require the observance of the laws of *kashrut*.

the same faith from different countries. Age, gender, race, sexuality and education, to name but a few factors, may also create difference. From an external perspective a group may appear, at first glance, to be uniform and easily quantifiable with identical beliefs and needs, however, an insider may see complexities, which render all stereotypes and taxonomies as meaningless.

Gensler's second fallacy the "Soft-Golden Rule Fallacy" builds upon his first reinterpretation of the Golden Rule (Gensler, 2012). The requirement to intuit the needs of the other before acting may lead to the assumption that we should never act against what others want, no matter how dangerous. Gensler, however, rejects this supposition, suggesting that if we determine that the identified needs are dangerous to his or her well being than we are not obligated by the Golden Rule to fulfill them. Thus, he posits, just because we intuit that a particular baby wants to put its finger in an electrical outlet, there is no requirement to fulfill this desire or allow the baby to do as he wishes.

The perception of danger, however, can be culturally – or even idiosyncratically – constrained. The belief, for example, that circumcision is harmful has led to attempts in California and other jurisdictions to render it illegal. Although there is good medical research that circumcision is either health neutral or even of benefit, the acceptance by adherents of the change in the law that circumcision may be harmful has challenged religious norms of both Judaism and Islam.

This reading of the Golden Rule is rendered even more complex in the context of faith. This was made clear to me at a prayer breakfast I attended several years ago, soon after the Vatican had issued a statement discouraging missionizing to the Jews. I was seated with a prominent evangelical minister and a Catholic bishop. The minister stated that the Catholic Church must hate the Jewish people. When the bishop expressed surprise, the minister explained that if you truly loved a people you would not allow them to be damned.

The minister believed that his faith was the only true way to achieve salvation, and that any one who follows another faith would be consigned to destruction or to Hell. Obviously such a punishment can be perceived as an eternal danger for adherents of other faiths. Gensler's resolution of the second fallacy would then be an encouragement, if not an obligation, to attempt to bring such persons to the "true faith" and thus saving their souls and giving them eternal life. Indeed, even the logic of the resolution of the first fallacy calls for the same reaction. If, following Gensler's logic, I was in their place and faced such a danger, I would want someone to save me from it.

Within the context of multi-faith both types of assumptions of danger can lead to a disruption, rather than enhancement, of inter-group relations. This suggests that blanket utilization of the Golden Rule may not be appropriate in these settings. Although Gensler is correct in identifying misinterpretations for the implementation of the Golden Rule, both resolutions he suggests are as challenging – at least in the context of multi-faith relations – as the identified fallacies. It is neither possible to make the imaginative leap to truly know the "other," nor to be absolutely objective as we determine, that which is dangerous to the well being of the "other."

Raimon Panikkar, an influential advocate of dialogue, use of the Golden Rule as a basis of his intra-faith interaction points to an additional challenge posed by the Golden Rule to inter-religious interaction (Panikkar, 1999). Panikkar suggests that the command, "to love another as oneself" demands that when we engage the other in dialogue we must move beyond acceptance of the humanity of the other, and even beyond non-judgmental acceptance of the other's ideas. Instead, he suggests, we must embrace the other's views as our own, and allow them to challenge and transform us (51). Herman Melville describes the logical conclusions of this form of interaction (built on the Golden Rule) in Moby Dick.

> *But what is worship? – to do the will of God – that is worship. And what is the will of God? – to do to my fellow man what I would have my fellow man to do to me – that is the will of God. Now, Queequeg is my fellow man. And what do I wish that this Queequeg would do to me? Why, unite with me in my particular Presbyterian form of worship. Consequently, I must then unite with him in his; ergo, I must turn idolater (Melville, 1967: 54).*

While this view has its attractions, in essence it is a denial of the authenticity of both parties, because there is an implicit idea that there is a truth to be found which perforce is transformative. Panikkar implicitly denies the legitimacy of remaining true to ones own traditions following the engagement in intra-religious dialogue.

Despite these challenges the "Golden Rule has become the one of the most pervasive narratives within interfaith discourse, suggesting that it is the uniting message of religion and is part of our planet's common language (Wattles, 1996: 189).[40] Indeed, proponents suggest that the Golden Rule should be the unifying ethic that brings humanity together, perhaps implying that this distilled "essential message" can form the basis not only of a global ethic but also of a global religion. Jeffrey Wattles' influential *The Golden Rule* concludes with just this suggestion (165-189). He suggests that it can be the "balm for an overly theological religious consciousness" that overrides the specifics of diverse religious traditions to create the "universal family of God" (185).

Is this narrative useful in the understanding, or even uniting (if this is considered an appropriate interfaith goal) diverse religions? Would a religion be inauthentic if it did not have a version of the Golden Rule? As noted above, the idea of the Golden Rule is a Western, especially Christian, religious concept.[41] This raises important question about the legitimacy of the search for it within other traditions. Indeed, the very search can be seen as an attempt either to say more or less benignly, "Isn't it wonderful that you are all like us (religions are really all the same)". Or, more dangerously, it can implicitly state, "We have the truth and we will find it or impose it wherever we go." Today in most cases the search for the Golden Rule appears to be an attempt to create comfort and to emphasize the unique rightness of our own traditions by finding ourselves in the "other."

There are numerous websites (and even more programs created by multi-faith organizations across the globe) dedicated to the idea that the Golden Rule, or more generically the "Law of Reciprocity" is the essential message of world religions.[42] Interestingly, while the websites examined

---

40   Wattles' book, *The Golden Rule* presents the most comprehensive discussion of the Golden Rule. It is examined both historically and philosophically. However, with the exception of a chapter examining the Golden Rule within Confucianism, the book focuses on development, understanding and critique of it in the western philosophic and religious traditions. Wattles book is quoted on many of the websites that present the Golden Rule as a uniting religious ethic (see, for example, www.scarboromissions.ca/golden_rule/index.php.

41   The essential Western focus on the Golden rules as the essence of the religious ethics (and indeed the essence of religion) is highlighted by Wattles book.

42   A Google search brought up more than a hundred websites celebrating the Golden Rule as the essential message of world religions. See, for example www.religioustolerance.org/reciproc.htm or www.scarboromissions.ca/Golden_rule/index.php. The Scarboro Mission, a Catholic organization, has made the Golden Rule a focus of its work. It produces a poster in several languages and its website contains a wide variety of Golden Rule programming ideas.

list up to twenty-one different versions of the Golden Rule two things become clear: the traditions claimed on these sites to express the same essential message are very different and often only the so-called "great religions" of the world (and also something listed under the generic term "native spirituality") are included.[43]

A perusal of the traditions included on these websites as versions of the Golden Rule is quite instructive in that the connections between the traditions grouped under this narrative are quite broad. Any statement (there is no indication of relative importance) from a religious tradition that in a general sense implies a connection between one person and another fits under the rubric of the Golden Rule.[44] Some of the traditions included require an active sense of responsibility, while others are more passive, requiring merely that one wish the other well. The Hindu entry, for example, states, "Do not do unto others what would cause pain if done unto you," while the Muslim entry reads, "Not one of you truly believes until you wish for others what you wish for yourself" (Scarboro Missions, 2000). Versions of the Golden Rule included in these lists are also both positive and negative, While the classic Christian formulation is positive, the most quoted Jewish one is negative, "That which is hateful to you, do not do to your fellow. That is the whole Torah; the rest is the

---

Interfaith programs utilizing the "Golden Rule narrative are widespread in North America. Two examples of these programs were developed in Arizona and Saskatchewan. The Arizona Interfaith Movement, for example, created (in conjunction with the State of Arizona) both a Golden Rule license plate and several other projects dedicated to the Golden Rule as the essential message of religion. Indeed, its mission expressly is to "build bridges of understanding … through the implementation of the Golden Rule" (http://www.interfaitharizona.com/). The Multi-Faith Saskatchewan organization also focused on the Golden Rule when it created a sacred space incorporating plaques inscribed with the Golden Rule in different religious traditions (http://www.multifaithsask.org/designated-sacred-space-project-2/#more-100)

43   While the religions included in the websites perused are somewhat diverse all include the so-called "great religions" with the addition of other ancient (e.g., Jainism or Confucianism) or early modern traditions (e.g., Baha'i and Unitarianism). None of the websites include any modern or new age traditions (the one exception is Wicca which is found on one of the websites).

44   Interestingly Wattles identifies this problem in his introduction (4). He suggests that activists have attempted identify the Golden Rule as the unifying message of world religions, yet, he notes, under closer examination it is clear that a rule which initially appeared similar may have very different formulations and implications in diverse religions.

explanation; go and learn" (Scarboro Missions, 2000). Other traditions seem to fit under the Golden Rule rubric in only the most tangential sense and may have been included for reasons other than the appropriateness of the association. The statement listed under the puzzlingly broad rubric of "native spirituality," for example, has little or nothing to do with reciprocity, at least between one human and another, "We are as much alive as we keep the earth alive" (Scarboro Missions, 2000).[45] Indeed, Wattles himself adds a further complication, noting that in some traditions the Golden Rule applies only to adherents, while in others it is interpreted more universally (Wattles, 4). The differences among traditions indicated by the formulations selected renders the entire narrative of the Golden Rule so broad as to be meaningless, and in actuality highlights the diversity found within world religious traditions.

The websites that attempt to present the Golden Rule, as the essential message of religion also create an artificially imposed hierarchy of values. While Judaism and Christianity both prioritize the law of reciprocity as the "great principle," or the Golden Rule, other traditions, which have a version of the law of reciprocity, may see it as important, but not the essential message of their tradition. This imposed hierarchy may prevent a true understanding of other traditions. Indeed, it may be impossible to authentically understand rules of reciprocity in other traditions if they are taken out of context.

It can be argued that despite these critiques that the Golden Rule narrative is harmless or even beneficial as it highlights a very positive and perhaps pervasive ethic. Yet how do we interpret religious traditions that do not enshrine a version of the "Golden Rule?" One anecdotal experience can illustrate the danger raised by this question. An early version of this chapter (including this question) was presented at an interfaith conference, which coincidentally was followed by a session highlighting Golden Rule projects around North America.[46] Following this second session, a Wiccan attendee stated that her tradition did not include a version of the Golden Rule, and that she felt both uncomfortable and excluded when people from outside her tradition insisted that it

---

[45] See also the Yoruba and Wiccan entries on the Religious Tolerance website, www.religioustolerance.org/reciproc.htm.

[46] NAIN Connect conference held in Salt Lake City in July 2010. NAIN (North American Interfaith Network) provides an umbrella for interfaith organizations in the United States and Canada.

did.[47] During a private discussion it became clear that this statement was of great concern to a board member of the organization sponsoring the conference. When asked why, she stated that if a religion did not have a version of the Golden Rule, than it was obviously not a "true" religion, as the Golden Rule was the essential revelation given us by God. As demonstrated by this anecdote, while Golden Rule attempts to create or impose unity, it has a dark side, in that it also can deem as illegitimate anything that falls outside its artificially constructed parameters. Religious traditions are diverse, with vastly differing histories, understandings of the divine (or even if there is a divine), True multi-faith harmony and positive relationships require that we recognize diversity and accept other traditions regardless of their acceptance of the Golden Rule.

---

47 The Wiccan Rede, "An it harm no one, do what thou wilt." Is included in the Golden Rule website, noted above. This is another example of the shoehorning of a very different ethic into the Golden Rule narrative. Though pushed by the moderator of the session to accept this identification, the Wiccan attendee at the conference was unwilling to make this jump.

IV

There is an Even Greater Principle

It may seem strange to some that the Golden Rule, narrative would trouble a rabbi, both as it was presented at the 1893 World's Parliament of Religions, and as it has been used subsequently as a central uniting message of interfaith interaction. Indeed, ancient Jewish figures as important as Hillel and Rabbi Akiba point to versions of the rule as the essence, or the "great principle," of Judaism. Yet, the sages were not unanimous in acceptance of this principle as the essence of Torah and many other texts are suggested. Indeed, even within one of the major Golden Rule texts, we are left at its conclusion with a very different "great principle," suggesting that the Golden Rule may be insufficient and that there is a more basic principle that underlies the Jewish world view.

Short attention span and sound bites are not only modern phenomena. Even in ancient times there was a realization that the system of commandments, and the variety of texts including the traditional Jewish library was hard to reduce to an easily understandable core. This led, as it does today, to attempts by various rabbis and thinkers to identify the basic essential traditions upon which the rest was based. This process is best summed up by a well-known text found in the Babylonian Talmud (Makkot 23b-24a) that examines a variety of biblical formulations in order to find the essence of Torah.[48]

> *Rabbi Simlai expounded: Six hundred and thirteen commandments were given to Moses, three hundred and sixty-five negative commandments (corresponding to the days of the year) and two hundred and*

---

48 The Babylonian Talmud, completed in the seventh century of the Common Era, is the most important creation of Rabbinic Judaism. It is a compendium of law and lore, which is still considered authoritative by traditional Judaism, and is seen by many as the product of divine oral revelation at Mt Sinai. Torah refers to the first five books of the Hebrew bible, and is believed by many to have been given, word for word, by God to Moses on Mt Sinai.

forty-eight positive commandments (corresponding to the bones of the human body)...[King] David came and established eleven [ethical principles] as the basis [for the six hundred and thirteen][49]... Isaiah came and established the basis upon six[50]...Micah came and established the basis upon three[51]...Isaiah came again and established the basis upon two[52]...Then Amos came and established the basis on one[53]...Rather [it was] Habakkuk who came and established them upon one, as it is said "The Righteous shall live by his faith."[54]

The essential message of Torah, established at the conclusion of this Talmudic text is very different than the Golden Rule.[55]

While one might think that it would be easy to isolate the first Jewish version of the Golden Rule within a particular verse in the Torah, and indeed many have pointed to Leviticus 19:18, "You shall love your neighbor as yourself," in actuality it is necessary to point to the entire

---

49   The eleven principles attributed to King David are derived from Psalm 15. "Lord, who may sojourn in Your tent, who may dwell on Your holy mountain? One who lives without blame (1), who does what is right (2), and in his heart acknowledges the truth (3); whose tongue is not given to evil (4); who has never done harm to his fellow (5), or borne reproach for [his acts towards] his neighbor (6); for whom a contemptible man is abhorrent (7), but who honors those who fear the Lord (8); who stands by his oath even to his hurt (9); who has never lent money at interest (10), or accepted a bribe against the innocent (11). One who acts thus shall never be shaken."

50   Isaiah's six principles are found in Is. 33:14-16. "Who of us can dwell with the devouring fire: who of us can dwell with the never-dying blaze? He who walks in righteousness (1), speaks uprightly (2), spurn's profit from fraudulent dealings (3), waves away a bribe instead of grasping it (4), stops his ears against listening to infamy (5), shuts his eyes against looking at evil (6). Such a one shall dwell in lofty security."

51   "He has told you, O man, what is good and what the Lord requires of you: only to do justice (1), and to love goodness (2), and to walk modestly with your God (3). (Micah 6:8)

52   "This said the Lord: Observe what is right (1) and do what is just (2)." (Is. 56:1)

53   "Thus said the Lord to the House of Israel: Seek me, and you will live (1)." (Amos 5:4).

54   Hab. 2:4.

55   Another similar Talmudic text which establishes a single verse as the essential principle is found on Berachot 63a, "Bar Kappara taught: which is the shortest verse upon which all the fundamentals of Torah depend. It is this, "In all your ways you must know Him, and He will straighten your paths" (Prov. 3:6)."

nineteenth chapter of Leviticus. This section of the Torah has been called the "Holiness Code," because it begins with the command "You shall be holy, for I, the Lord your God am holy" (19:1). This stirring evocation is followed by a series of *mitzvot* (commandments) both ritual and ethical. While some deal with prohibitions against idolatry, sacrifice and dietary rules, most focus on basic human relations. Among other laws, the list includes both a command for the fair provision of justice and the obligation to provide food for the disadvantaged of the community. Yet, most interestingly, twice in the list we are commanded to love others as ourselves. While verse 18 commands us to "love our neighbor," the *mitzvah* in verse 34 is "love the stranger." Taken as a whole, the entire chapter suggests that holiness is found within the community, as we observe the cultic rituals, but more importantly as we create a society based on respect for all its members.

Despite the fact that within Jewish sources the classical formulation of the Golden Rule, ultimately has its roots in the Leviticus, the most quoted version of the rule is derived from the Babylonian Talmud (Shabbat 31a).

> *[A Gentile] came before Hillel [and asked to be converted on the condition that Hillel would teach him the entire Torah while standing on one foot]. Hillel said to him, "That which is hateful to you, do not do to your fellow. This is the entire Torah the rest is an elaboration. Go and learn.*

This text forms part of a series of incidents where a non-Jew approaches Hillel and Shammai (the two most prominent rabbinic figures in the period just before the beginning of the Common Era) purportedly to convert to Judaism. In each text the gentile presents a difficult or controversial challenge, to which Shammai responds by chasing him away, while Hillel provides an answer that draws him in.

It is interesting that in providing its "essence" Hillel chooses not to quote the Torah directly, and instead presents a paraphrase of the original. Indeed, his answer transforms the Leviticus text from a positive to a negative commandment. Both the entire concept of such a limited "essence," and this transformation were troubling to some later rabbis. While the text seemed to be inclusive of all the miztvot between one human and an other, where, they ask, were all of the obligations vis-à-vis humanity and God? Rashi (Rabbi Shlomo Yitzhaki, 1040-1105) suggests that either Hillel was providing a shorthand response, since most of the laws in the Torah are ethical, or that "your fellow" also includes the concept "that which is hateful to God" – adding to Hillel's dictum all the ritual as well as ethical mitzvot.

The Maharsha (Samuel Eidels, 1555-1631) examines Hillel's transformation of the text from the positive to the negative, suggesting that the obligation to love one's neighbor is primarily defined by what one should not do another human being, rather than what someone should do. Eidels may be suggesting that it is more difficult to know what another person wants or needs, than what will be harmful to them.

The positive version of the Golden Rule, as found in Leviticus 19:18, is utilized directly by a later generation of rabbis and it is in this context that it is called the *klal gadol*, the great principle, of the Torah. This text, found in the early rabbinic midrash Sifra (89b), two rabbis, Akiba, and Ben Azzai, present their various opinions about the "*klal gadol*," the great – that is to say the guiding fundamental – principle that shapes Torah and Judaism. [56] As Hillel did, these rabbis also exclude theological principles, dealing with the nature of God, or of God's connection with humanity. Rather the rabbis also identify texts that deal with relationships between human beings.[57] Both rabbis choose single verses from the Torah that they believe represent the underlying theme of the whole.

> "You shall love your neighbor as yourself." (Leviticus 19:18) Rabbi Akiba said: This is the fundamental principle of the Torah. Ben Azzai said: "This is the book of the generations of man." (Genesis 5:1) is a fundamental principle superior to this (the verse selected by Rabbi Akiba)."

While Rabbi Akiba's answer is similar to one given in an earlier generation by Hillel the Elder, Rabbi Akiba's formulation is a positive *mitzvah*, while Hillel's is negative. As noted by the Maharsha there is a significant difference between the negative and positive formulations. Indeed,

---

56   See also *Genesis R., Bereshit* 24:7. Interestingly in this text Ben Azzai's principle is included first, and it is Rabbi Akiva's, which is identified as superior.

57   The stress on the primary importance of the relationship between human beings over the relationship of humanity with God is also found in texts dealing with the Yom Kippur. *Mishnah, Yoma* 8:9 reminds us that we must first repent from sins against other human beings before we can be forgiven for sins committed against God.

it is difficult to equate the two as statements of the same Golden Rule. The positive formulation implies that one can know within one's self how another person should be treated. If, for example I am convinced of the absolute rightness of my belief, then I have not only the right, but also the obligation to attempt to impose it on the other. The negative formulation, on the other hand includes only those things that one is forbidden to do to another. So, for example, just as I don't wish to be proselytized, so too I am forbidden to proselytize.[58]

There is also an ambiguity found within both Akiba and Hillel's statements. In both cases, while the text chosen teaches that the essence of the Torah is the obligation to treat others well – or at least not badly – the word neighbor, or fellow, is left undefined. Does this obligation extend to all humanity or is it limited to fellow Jews? Does it extend to people in far off counties, or is it limited to one's immediate neighborhood? While it is possible to answer both these questions in a very liberal way, the contrary is also a legitimate answer to the questions.

These Golden Rule traditions are insufficient to solve the ambiguity, it is therefore necessary to go back to the original context as found in Leviticus. As noted, both rabbis quote (or allude to) the same verse, Leviticus 19:18. While the Holiness Code, Leviticus 19, contains a variety of laws from the ritual to the secular, which the Biblical author states are necessary to create a holy society, it does not directly define the concept of holiness. Rather, it provides a hint of its meaning, stating at the very beginning, "You shall be Holy, for I, the Lord your God, am holy" (Leviticus 19:2) The verse suggests that we achieve holiness when we model our lives, to the best of our abilities after our perception of God's actions in the world.

This concept of holiness, as derived from imitation of God's actions, is found throughout rabbinic literature. One Talmudic text, *Sotah* 14a, describes God's activities in several biblical stories as models for our behavior.[59]

---

58 The negative formulation creates an ethical quandary of its own. If I don't like being helped, then perhaps I am not required to help others. This underlies the insufficiency of any version of the golden rule, negative or positive, in creating a comprehensive and usable ethical system. The "Holiness Code", taken as a whole, and the midrashim adduced at the end of this chapter introduce motivations for our responsibilities to our fellow humans.

59 See also Sifre Deuteronomy, *Ekev*, which uses the thirteen attributes of

As God clothes the naked (Adam and Eve), you should clothe the naked. As the Holy One visited the sick (Abraham, following his circumcision), you should visit sick. As the Holy One comforted mourners (Isaac, after the death of Abraham), you to should comfort mourners. As the Holy One buried the dead (Moses was buried by God), you should bury the dead.

The principle of *imitatio dei* leads to a very broad interpretation of neighbor or fellow. The biblical God is portrayed not only as the god and creator of Israel but also as the creator and ruler of all humanity. This is most tellingly portrayed by the prophet Amos (9:7), "To me, O Israelites, you are just like the Ethiopians – declares the Lord. True, I brought Israel up from the land of Egypt, but also the Philistines from Caphtor and the Arameans from Kir." The prophet reminds us that God is the redeemer of humanity, not just the Jewish people. It is therefore not a large jump to interpret "neighbor" in the widest possible sense.

This interpretation is also strengthened by a perusal of other laws found within the same section of the Torah. Leviticus 19:34 states, "The stranger who resides with you should be treated the same as the native born, and you shall love him as yourself; for you were strangers in the land of Egypt." This verse teaches us that our experiences should lead us to the broadest interpretation of "neighbor", a category that clearly should include Jew and non-Jew.

The use of the term stranger in Leviticus 19:34 also suggests a difficulty with the Golden Rule. While there is a possibility that one can, to some extent, foresee the needs of one's neighbor or fellow, the strangeness of the "other" renders this impossible. We should not assume that our needs, desires or understandings of the world should be the same as people coming from disparate lands or traditions. It is for this reason that if forced, I would choose this formulation rather than the one found in Leviticus 19:18.

Obligations to the stranger, and the necessity of creating a world where care is provided for strangers and indeed all who are disadvantaged, forms an important refrain throughout the Jewish tradition. Judaism has always stressed that experience is the great educator. When Jews look back at our history we are obligated not to see it just as events in the past, but rather as events that we ourselves participate in, and which give

---

God (derived from Exodus 34:6) as a model for human behavior.

us insights into how to shape our lives. Thus, on Passover the Mishnah teaches that each of us must see ourselves as coming forth from Egypt (*Pes.* 10:5). This imperative – that we ourselves were part of the events – strengthens the commandments that are based on experience.

Perhaps the most important set of commandments built on experience are those that stem from the time that our people were slaves in Egypt. The Torah teaches that this experience should not teach bitterness, or even hatred of the Egyptians, rather we are commanded to learn compassion, and obligation for those outside the community. "You shall not wrong the stranger or oppress him, for you were strangers in the land of Egypt" (*Exodus* 22:20). We, as a people, knew what it was to be oppressed as strangers in a strange land. We knew that the stranger was easily oppressed in the ancient – as well as the modern world, since he did not have a family or community on which to depend. Therefore experience – and God – demands that we treat the stranger with respect and even love.

The importance of this law is indicated by the number of times that it is mentioned in the Torah. The rabbis of the Talmud count thirty-six occurrences of commandments based on the obligation to remember the stranger and treat him/her well (*Baba Metzia.* 59b).[60] Indeed, the obligation to the stranger goes well beyond the avoidance of oppression. In addition to the negative formulations of "not wronging him," (*Leviticus* 19:33) and "not subverting his rights" (*Deuteronomy* 24:17) we are also positively commanded to "rejoice with the stranger," (*Deuteronomy* 16:11) and to "love him as yourself" (*Leviticus* 19:34). In addition to an insight gained from our history, this, perhaps, is a reminder of our common humanity: a concept, which Ben Azzi stressed.

Ben Azzai's "great principle" avoids ambiguity, reminding us at once of the common origin of humanity. His verse, "this is the book of the generations of Adam [and Eve]" is all-inclusive, including all humanity or indeed all of creation as it reminds us that God is the creator of not only Adam and Eve but the entire world. Indeed, in a real sense, it can be seen as a response to the ambiguity found in Rabbi Akiba's statement. Rabbi Akiba leaves us questioning who is our neighbor. Ben Azzai

---

60   The Talmud states that this injunction is mentioned either 36 or 46 times. While it translates *ger* according to its own usage as "convert," the Torah itself, however, had no notion of conversion to Judaism. A better translation of the term might be resident alien, or stranger – as it is rendered in the J.P.S. translation.

answers, everyone is your neighbor, because within the biblical understanding of creation, "the generations of Adam" include every human being, each of us is a descendant of Adam and Eve.

Ben Azzai rejects the idea that the Torah allows us to treat one group of humans well while mistreating others. He also rejects the idea that one group of humans is superior or inferior to any others. Each human is important and each has the same status because we are all descended from the same parents. An elaboration of Ben Azzai's dictum, found in the rabbinic midrash, Bereshit Rabba 24:7, that builds upon the concept of shared humanity is found following Ben Azzai's suggested "great principle." This addition also solves another ambiguity found within the Golden Rule.

> *That you should not say, since I am despised let my neighbor be similarly despised, since I am cursed, let my neighbor be similarly cursed. Said Rabbi Tanhuma: If you act this way, know whom you are despising, "In the likeness of God made He him." (Genesis 5:1)*

Rabbi Tanhuma teaches that the obligation to treat others well is based, therefore, not only on our common ancestry, but also on the commonality of being created in God's image which is also shared by all humanity. To him, therefore, it would be not only be a societal crime to mistreat another human being, but it would be blasphemous as well.

Ben Azzai's stress on the brotherhood of all humanity is not an isolated example of this concept. Rather, an examination of many other rabbinic texts dealing with creation furthers both the concept of universal kinship, and also of the importance of each individual as a unique human being. There are many midrashim that examine human beings vis-à-vis creation. These texts both discuss humanity in relation to the rest of creation, as well as identify the messages behind the specifics of human creation.

Perhaps the most interesting question examined in several texts found in the Talmud (Sanhedrin 37a) fits within both these categories. Why, the rabbis ask, was one human being – Adam – created while all other animals were created in their multitudes? The rabbinic answers to this question support the centrality in Torah and Judaism of Ben Azzai's principal, the universal brotherhood of humanity.

One answer, made famous by *Schindler's List*, clearly establishes the importance of each human being, no matter who he or she is. The Talmud asks, "Why does the Torah state that one human being was created? To teach that if one saves a single human life it is as if one has saved the entire world."[61] To the author of this statement, each of us represents a whole world of potential, both within ourselves and within our potential descendants. Therefore, each of us is important and unique.

The Talmud also adds the converse of this statement, reminding us that "if we kill a single human being it is as if we are destroying the entire world." This text reminds us that each of us has an almost universal importance and potential. There are things that only we can accomplish, and each of us can be a parent to an "entire world" of future human beings, all of whom may have great things to contribute to humanity and the world. Therefore, we have an obligation to respect and see worth within each human being.

This uniqueness of each human is also stressed in a rabbinic parable interpreting the concept of creation in the image of God.

> *The greatness of the Holy One, blessed be He, is thus demonstrated. For, when a man mints coins from one die, each one is the same as the rest. But, when the Supreme King of Kings, the Holy One, blessed be He, coined each person with the die of Adam, each one is different.* (Bereshit Rabba 24:7)

Each human being is unique, yet each of us is also created in the image of God. Therefore, as Ben Azzai teaches, if we despise or mistreat any human it is as if we were also despising or mistreating God.

The text from the Talmud adds an additional explanation for the creation of a single human, which stresses even more explicitly the necessity, stemming from creation, of accepting and embracing diversity, "Man was created alone for the sake of peace. So that one man would not say to another, my father was greater than your father." In this text the Talmud explicitly rejects any view of superiority between the peoples of the world.[62] These texts also underlie an important ambiguity, as discussed above, with the Golden Rule. If each of us is unique, then it is impossible and indeed arrogant for any person to believe that he or she knows what

---

61   The Talmudic dictum on the value of saving a human life is also echoed with an identical formulation in the *Qur'an*, 2:190.

62   Another rabbinic text also stresses the importance of diversity by stressing the common nature of humanity, and its connection with the rest of creation. "Rabbi Meir used to say, "The dust used to create Adam was gathered from the four corners of the earth." (*Sanhedrin* 38b)

is best for another. Indeed, if a "great principle" needs to be identified, than in essence, these texts demonstrate that respect for human diversity is truly the "great principle" of the Torah.

One further text, found in the Sifre on Deuteronomy (Sofetim 187), an early work of rabbinic Midrash, also suggests that there are Jewish essential messages that transcend the Golden Rule. Indeed, this text claims that "Love your neighbor as yourself," is a light, perhaps less important, commandment.

> *He who violates a light commandment will ultimately violate a heavy (more stringent) one. He who violates, 'Love your neighbor as yourself,' will ultimately violate, 'You shall not hate your brother in your heart, and you shall not take vengeance nor bear any grudge' and even 'He shall live with you' (Leviticus 25:35), till at the end he will come to shedding blood.*

This text suggests that the Golden Rule, is not the essential message of the tradition, but rather it acts as a fence[63] preventing us from breaking more important commandments.

Far from being the unanimous choice as the essence of Judaism the Golden Rule is one principle among many others contending to play that role. Indeed, in the one text that highlights it as the "great principle" the rabbis, themselves, undermine its centrality by claiming, "there is a principle greater than this." Ultimately, within the Jewish tradition, texts that highlight the common creation of humanity in the image of God, and the uniqueness of each human being appear more important in underlying the world view of the tradition.

---

63 Within the rabbinic tradition many laws were established with the purpose of preventing people from breaking more important (most often Biblical) injunctions.

V

A New Dialectic

ALL INTERRELIGIOUS CONTACT IS A FORM OF DIALOGUE, whether formal or informal. Yet, dialogue – especially in its formal manifestations – has been constrained by a sense that transformation, especially in the realization of the narrative of "religious essentialism," is necessary, else the dialogue would be a failure engendering, it is believed, bad feelings which would exacerbate difficult relations between groups. In most cases, therefore, interfaith dialogues are set up with a carefully arranged choice of topics to ensure success. Difficult or controversial issues are often avoided, as there is a fear that controversial opinions will alienate attendees who desire "essential messages" that mirror their own beliefs. These dialogues, and indeed most multi-faith programming, follow a Hegelian mode of dialectic, where the synthesis of "religious essentialism" is most often the intended end result of the dialogue. Are our traditions indeed all at essence the same? Are the differences between us important? Are there different "truths" about the nature of the world and the divine? These questions challenge the status quo and suggest that perhaps a mode of non-Hegelian dialectic would be more fruitful in creating a more authentic mode of interfaith acceptance understanding.

The dialectic found both within Jewish rabbinic sources and within the Jain tradition may provide just such a useful counter model of dialectic for interfaith interaction.[64] While this model comes out of two particular world views I would contend that it is generalizable to our present context.

While the Hegelian dialectic ending as it does with one synthesis or answer – in this context the meta-narrative of religious essentialism – fits with the modernist world view, the Jain and Talmudic dialectics, with their respect for the contingent and contextual, are post-modern in their approach to the rejection of any grand narrative of "religious essentialism," or universal religious "truth." The classic dialectic – with its steps of

---

64 The Jain tradition is an ancient religion that developed in India sometime during the ninth and the sixth centuries B.CE.

thesis, antithesis, and synthesis – is geared at finding the "ultimate truth." The Jain and Talmudic dialectics have a very different goal, namely to leave room for a multiplicity of truths.[65]

Based on this model of dialectic, interfaith dialogue would therefore no longer be concerned with identifying the kernel of truth, "the essential message," which unites all religions. Instead, it would aim to value difference and diversity of participants and traditions. Both the analysis above and the model suggest that the search for the "essential message" blinds us from seeing the "other" as he or she truly is, allowing us only to see them within our own contingent and contextual "correct answers."

Talmudic Dialectic

There is a well-known Jewish joke, which captures, effectively, the concept of "absolute truth" within a Jewish context.

> *A new rabbi comes to a well-established congregation. Every week on the Sabbath, an argument erupts during the service. When it comes time to recite the Shema prayer (the one major creedal statement accepted as authoritative by the entire Jewish community), half of the congregation stands and the other half sits. The half who stand say, "Of course we stand for the Shema. It's the credo of Judaism. Throughout history, thousands of Jews have died with the words of the Shema on their lips." The half who remain seated say, "No, tradition states that if you are seated when you get to the Shema you remain seated."*
>
> *The people who are standing yell at the people who are sitting, "stand up!" while the people who are sitting yell at the people who are standing, "sit down!" It's destroying the whole decorum of the service, and driving the new rabbi crazy. Finally, the rabbi learns that a 98-year-old man who was a founding member of the congregation lives at a nearby home for the aged. So, in accordance with Talmudic tradition, the rabbi appoints a*

---

65   The reader may note that the texts examined below discuss matters of ritual rather than belief. This reflects the fact that traditional Judaism has often been described as an orthopraxy rather than an orthodoxy. Belief within rabbinic Judaism is very idiosyncratic and therefore contingent and contextual, while ritual (commandment) is more structured and communal.

delegation of three, one who stands for the Shema, one who sits, and the rabbi himself, to interview the man.

They enter his room, and the man who stands for the Shema rushes over to the old man and says, "Wasn't it the tradition in our synagogue to stand for the Shema?" "No," the old man answers in a weak voice. "That wasn't the tradition." The other man jumps in excitedly. "Wasn't it the tradition in our synagogue to sit for the Shema?" "No," the old man says. "That wasn't the tradition."

At this point, the rabbi cannot control himself. He cuts in angrily. "I don't care what the tradition was! Just tell them one or the other. Do you know what goes on in services every week — the people who are standing yell at the people who are sitting, the people who are sitting yell at the people who are standing—" The old man interrupts the rabbi and loudly says, "That was the tradition."

This joke reflects both the possibility of a simultaneous existence of a multiplicity of truths, as well as difficulty that human beings have in accepting this possibility. As will be seen below, this joke recapitulates an ancient rabbinic argument.[66]

A Talmudic argument rarely follows the steps of a classic dialectic, with its neat format of thesis, antithesis and synthesis; instead there are often numerous antitheses, and almost never an explicit synthesis. It is left to readers to determine which answer is correct, and that decision is always contingent and contextual. Indeed, even an answer that may be chosen as "correct" in one generation can be rejected by another, or indeed even in the same period, but in a different community. The Talmudic dialectic implies at least the possibility that all sincere answers, contradictory or not, are aspects of "truth."

The possibility of a multiplicity of truths is explicitly noted within a Talmudic foundational myth included in both the Jerusalem Talmud (Berachot 1:7, 3b) and in the Babylonian Talmud (Eruvin 13b). In the text from the Je-

---

66 This joke may seem somewhat far-fetched, yet often life imitates art. I once applied for a rabbinic position in the UK. In this congregation a small group always stood for the *shema* because this had been the custom of a previous (now deceased) rabbi, while the remainder of the congregation sat for the recitation of the prayer. When new rabbis visited the community both sides always attempted to gain their support.

rusalem Talmud, the House of Hillel and the House of Shammai (two major schools of thought in the early rabbinic period) argue for three years about the correct way to say the Shema. The House of Hillel says it should always be said while seated and the House of Shammai says that in the morning it should be said while standing up.[67] At the conclusion of the passage a heavenly voice (Bat Kol) says, "These (words) and these (words) are both words of the living God. But the halakhah (law) is according to the House of Hillel." The text shows that all sides in discussions and arguments for the sake of heaven speak with the words of God. The text adds, "the law is according to the House of Hillel," merely to enable people at that time (contingent and contextual) to know how they were expected to act.

The text from the Babylonian Talmud is very similar to the text in the Jerusalem Talmud. The main difference of interest here is the conclusion. After stating that the law is according to the House of Hillel, the text adds an explanation for this decision.

> *If both [the words of the House of Hillel and the House of Shammai] are "the words of the living God," why did the House of Hillel merit that the law be according to their opinions? It was because they were gentle and kind, and quoted the words of the House of Shammai when they gave their own decision. They even put the words of the House of Shammai before their own words (T.B. Eruvin 13b).*

The Babylonian Talmud suggests that Hillel's opinion was chosen as correct for his time because he was willing to honestly present Shammai's view before his own, even though Shammai's "truth" was different from his own. Despite the fact that one side in the argument is chosen as expressing the law this does not mean that the other arguments can never be followed, even if, as in this case, God seemingly renders the decision.[68] The law, and future decisions about it, are given to humanity.

These texts also suggest a significant transformation in both the concepts of revelation and human decision-making where authority is no

---

67   Bet Shammai bases its argument on the verse, "you shall speak of them (i.e. recite the Shema) when you lie down and you rise up." (Deuteronomy. 6:6) Bet Shammai deduces that in the evening you should recite the Shema while seated (or reclining) and in the morning it should be recited while standing. Bet Hillel, on the other hand, claims that these only refer to the times the Shema should be recited and have no bearing on how the Shema should be recited.

68   On the same page of Eruvin quoted above (13b) God is said to have shown Moses forty-nine ways to make every issue permitted and forty-nine ways to make every issue forbidden.

longer universal, but is rather contingent and contextual. Indeed they are thus strong rejections of "religious essentialism." They suggest that the ongoing decision-making process is itself one of revelation. Although there is a mythological construct that the "revelation" is Sinaitic in origin, they allow a continuous process of decision-making – with the possibility and even likelihood of diverse answers – to be given the authority of the "original" revelation.

The possibility of differing correct answers, and a rejection of "absolute truth" is demonstrated clearly in the argument between the sages and Rabbi Eliezer (T.B. *Baba Metzia* 59b) concerning the *kashrut* of the oven of Aknai. In the text, the rabbis examine whether an oven comprised of separate tiles could be considered *kosher*. Rabbi Eliezer claims that the oven is acceptable, while the other sages claim that it is not.[69]

> *On that day R. Eliezer brought forward every imaginable argument, but they did not accept them. He said to them: "If the law is as I say, let this carob tree prove it!" Thereupon the tree was torn a hundred cubits out of its place — other say, four hundred cubits. "Proof cannot be brought from a carob tree," they responded. Then he said: "If the Law is as I say, let the stream of water prove it," whereupon the stream flowed backward. "No proof can be brought from a stream," they retorted. Then he said, "If the law is with me, let the walls of the academy prove it," whereupon the walls began to fall. But R. Joshua reproved them, saying: "When scholars are engaged in a legal dispute, what right have you to interfere?" Hence they did not fall, but in honor of R. Eliezer they are still standing inclined.*

The Talmud implies that R. Eliezer began with a series of arguments that should have established that his opinion was correct — indeed, he was considered to be the expert on the subject. Only when the majority refused to accept these arguments — implicitly reaching the *wrong* de-

---

69   The implication of the text seems to be that R. Eliezer in an "absolute" sense is correct. This is indicated both by the heavenly voice and perhaps by the language used to describe the other sages' arguments. The Talmud states, "they encompassed it with arguments as a snake and proved it unclean." The Aramaic for snake is a word play on the name of the owner of the oven. The rabbis are perhaps making a double allusion by this pun. A snake winds itself around an object, suggesting perhaps winding and convoluted arguments. It also may allude to the snake mentioned in *Eruvin* 13b discussed above. Ultimately, however the text rejects the concept of "absolute truth."

cision — did he resort to a series of miracles. When these too were not accepted, R. Eliezer calls on God to establish his claim.

> *Again he said to them: "If the law is as I say, let it be proved from heaven!" Whereupon a Bat Kol (a voice from heaven) said, "Why do you dispute with R. Eliezer, seeing that the law is always in accordance with his rulings?" But R. Joshua arose and said: "It is not in heaven."*

While the *Bat Kol* establishes that even God holds that R. Eliezer's answer is correct, this is countered by the statement "It (the Torah/law) is not in heaven."[70] The text concludes with the following explanation of this statement:

> *What did he (R. Joshua) mean by this? R. Jeremiah said, 'The Torah was already given at Mt. Sinai, and we now no longer listen to heavenly voices, as it is said in the Torah, 'after the majority are you to decide.'*[71]

The text then concludes with an interesting coda.

> *Rabbi Nathan met Elijah the Prophet and said to him, 'What did God do in that hour (at the time the Bat Kol was rejected)?' Elijah replied, 'God laughed and said, 'My children have conquered me, My children have conquered me.'*

The ramifications of this text are quite dramatic. It not only affirms the right of the sages in each generation to make decisions about the law, it also shows that despite the voice from heaven – and indeed with God's explicit support – it reaffirms that there is not one correct answer within Jewish law. Rather, the law of a generation is a product of the decisions and discussions of the sages in that generation.

The text can also be seen as an expression of a rabbinic debate on the nature of Jewish law and the possibility of change and development. Rabbi Eliezer represents the view that the law is similar in nature to a revealed text. That is to say, that it can be quantified listed, and exactly

---

70 Rabbi Joshua's challenge to the *Bat Kol* comes from Deuteronomy 30:12.

71 This interpretation based on Exodus 23:2. Interestingly, this statement is based on a deliberate misreading of the biblical text. The first words of the verse are omitted. The entire verse actually reads, "You should not follow the multitude to do evil."

determined, and that it represents a single "absolute truth." His view precludes the possibility of change since he holds that the exact revealed law can be established. The rabbis, on the other hand, represent the view that the law is not fixed, but rather is established through discussion and consensus among the sages in a contingent and contextual way. The view accepts, and even enshrines the possibility of a multiplicity of correct answers, since the understanding (and revelation) of the law is left to the sages and not to God.

The Jewish tradition views all answers as contingent and contextual. The *Mishnah*, an ancient and authoritative source, enshrines the possibility of differing answers in differing communities and times.

> *Why is the minority opinion recorded together with the majority opinion, since the Law is according to the majority? It is recorded so that if some court favors the minority opinion and decides in accordance with it, no other court may overturn the decision of that court, except if it is greater than the earlier court in wisdom and number (Eduyyot 1:5).*

Here, the *Mishnah* affirms the right of future courts to choose the minority opinion as law, even though the majority of the sages of the *Mishnah* were opposed to it. The minority opinions are preserved, therefore, to enable future courts to decide which opinion is correct, just as the sages of *Mishnah* had the choice as to which opinion was the law. Commenting on this *Mishnah*, medieval rabbi, Samson of Sens (twelfth century) goes so far as to say,

> *Even though the minority opinion was not accepted in the earlier time, and the majority did not agree with it, when the later generation arises and its majority agrees with the minority position, the law ought to be as they say, for the entire Torah was given to Moses with valid arguments for declaring unclean and valid arguments for declaring pure. (Commentary on Eduyyot 1:5)*

Jewish law, therefore, does not represent only one opinion, even that of the majority. But rather in each generation Jews must confront the major issues, and if necessary adopt minority opinions. This diversity within law and the ability for particular laws to change from age to age clearly rejects the concept of a single "absolute truth." Even religious truth is seen within the Jewish tradition as contingent and contextual.

This sense of contextuality is also stressed in the rabbinic process of *halakhic* (traditional Jewish legal) decision-making. For the rabbis the "law" in truth was not a list of laws, but rather a process by which the law of a particular time could be determined. The *halakhah* rejoices in its potential for diversity. A well-known text states that a rabbinic student was ordained only when he was able to prove in one hundred different ways that a snake (a prohibited food according to the dietary laws) was permissible to be eaten (T. B. *Eruvin* 13b). While Jewish practice may never have allowed the eating of a serpent, it is clear that the rabbinic tradition required that its students have the ability to be creative and to formulate and argue new approaches to the *halakhah*.

The very fact that a multiplicity of opinions are presented within the texts, especially the *Mishnah* and *Gamara*, demonstrates that *halakhah* does not have one correct answer, but rather admits the possibility of change. This point is also strongly emphasized in a text mentioned above, *Eruvin* 13b. This text suggests that for every decision in *halakhah* there are an equal number of arguments for all other possible decisions.

An examination of just one of the *halakhah's* fundamental principles demonstrates its scope for change and development and the importance it places on contextuality. In his investigation of the *halakhic* process, Rabbi Joel Roth states that the *sine qua non* of the *halakhah* is the principal that "a judge must be guided by what he sees"(Roth, 1986: 83).[72] Judges are commanded to base their judgments on the needs of their time and on the specifics of the case before them, rather than on the decisions of the past. Rabbi Roth asserts that this statement not only gives judges and *poskim* (interpreters of the law) the right to exercise judicial discretion, but it also demands that they exercise that right (85). If judges and *poskim* fail to examine the law according to the needs and realities of their own times, then the *halakhah* would cease to be either functional or relevant. The Jewish legal tradition needs to remain contextual in order to survive.

The rabbis do recognize that there are wrong as well as right answers. Their criteria, however, are somewhat different than those found within the western dialectic. They are based on motivation rather than a concept that an "absolute truth" is out there, waiting to be found. *Mishnah Avot* (5:19) states, "A controversy for the sake of heaven will have lasting value,

---

72 Roth demonstrates the ubiquity of the principal throughout the Talmud, see, for example, Niddah 20b, Sanhedrin 6b and Bava Batra 130b.

but a controversy not for the sake of heaven will not endure." An example of each type of argument is then adduced. The arguments of Hillel and Shammai (see the example found above) are an example of "an argument for the sake of heaven", while the rebellion of Korah and his followers, challenging Moses and Aaron's authority (see Numbers 16) is an "argument not for the sake of heaven" – because it was presumably an attempt to seize power based on ego, and against the will of God. The text suggests that any opinion based on a sincere desire to understand the divine will is a "truth," while arguments based on ego and a desire for power are not.

The potential for an ongoing dialogue and a open-ended dialectic is indicated in every traditional edition of major Jewish texts from the Bible to the Talmud, midrash and medieval codes. In a recent book, Rabbi Daniel Gordis described the Talmudic page as a "dialogue" across the generations (Gordis, 1995: 94-96). Nearly every generation of scholars of the Common Era (until the nineteenth century) is represented on the page and engages in dialogue and conversation about the possible meanings of the text, and the nature of Judaism and *halakhah*.

The center of each page includes the basic text of the *Talmud*, often including both the *Mishnah* (completed in the third century, but including discussion from the first two hundred years of the Common Era) and the *Gamara* (completed in the sixth century including discussions from mishnaic times and until its completion). It is within these texts that the debate on the nature of *halakhah* begins. The *Mishnah* generally includes simple statements of the law, with little expansion or explanation. That is not to say, however, that the *Mishnah* presents only one view. Rather, the *Mishnah* often includes a variety of views, and rarely will state which view is authoritative.[73] The *Gamara*, placed after each section of *Mishnah*, continues and broadens the debate. It may explain, and accept or reject the approaches found in the *Mishnah*, and it may even bring other possible answers not found there.

The commentaries found around the sides of the page also serve to demonstrate that the concept of open-ended dialectic exemplifies the *halakhic* tradition. Each generation of commentators felt free to present their understandings of the text and to disagree, when necessary, with the commentators that came before them. The fact that the disagree-

---

73 The *Gamara* and other later sources developed rules to determine which part of the *Mishnah* expressed the Law. But these were not always followed. Essentially any statement from the *Mishnah* could be taken as an expression of the law.

ments are printed together implicitly expresses the concept that there may not be one correct answer or interpretation.

The debate on the nature of *halakhah*, as represented by the page of Talmud is not, however, one sided, representing only those who believe in the diversity of acceptable interpretations. Expression of the desire to clearly state the *halakhah* as a presentable list of laws is also represented. The outer margin of each page of Talmud includes a cross reference to the major codes (thus allowing the reader to see which opinion is authoritative) called *Ein Mishpat Ner Mitzvah*. Even here, however, diversity is implied, since there is no guarantee, or even likelihood, that *halakhic* rulings of the major codes will agree on the subject under discussion. Thus, by its very nature, the design of the Talmud, and other Jewish texts admits and even welcomes diversity and open-ended dialectic. With each generational addition and with each difference of opinion, the possibility and acceptability diversity is celebrated and institutionalized.

The Jain Model

The Jain tradition grew out of ancient Hinduism between the ninth and sixth centuries Before the Common Era. Early Jain masters rejected certainties, and called on their followers to realize that all truths need to be viewed from a multiplicity of perspectives. This teaching, still central to the tradition, is exemplified in a Jain story, which now also has variants in other eastern traditions.

> *Once a King brought six blind men together and asked them to determine what an elephant was like by feeling different parts of the elephant's body. The blind man who felt a leg said, 'the elephant is like a pillar'; the one who felt the tail said, 'the elephant is like a rope'; the one who felt the trunk said, 'the elephant is like a tree branch'; the one who felt the ear said, 'the elephant is like a hand fan'; the one who felt the belly said, 'the elephant is like a wall'; and the one who felt the tusk said, 'the elephant is like a solid pipe.' Each one insisted that they alone were correct. The king then explained to them: 'all of you are right. Each one of you described a different truth about the elephant.' (Jain World)*

This seemingly simple story, stemming from the Jain tradition, exemplifies the belief that differing perceptions of the world lead to differing views of the truth.

The Jain tradition enshrines three principles, *anekantavada* (non-one-sidedness), *nayavada* (perspectives) and *syadvada* (the maybe doctrine), which encapsulate modes of understanding the world. Taken together these have been called the Jain "doctrines of relativity" (Lang, 2009: 117). These three approaches to the world are considered to be essential to lead a soul on the path of spiritual liberation. The story of 'The Elephant and the Blind Men," exemplifies these, teaching the realization that 'truth' is not absolute, but rather is contingent and contextual.

Anekantavada, examines the nature of being, suggesting that objects are simultaneously finite and infinite. Since all objects are not only finite but also infinite both in their qualities and modes of existence, it is impossible to grasp them in all their aspects and manifestations. *Nayavada*, is a doctrine of perspective, which is built on the ramifications of *anekantavada*. Since every object is infinitely complex, each object can be known from a variety of contradictory perspectives – e.g. that it is infinite yet finite — referred to as *nayas*. While each *naya* is a true, each is perforce only a limited description of the object. The third principle *Syadvada*, has been called the "maybe doctrine." Given the realization that the complexity of reality and the law of perspectives limit every attempt to describe the world, *Syadvada* requires the addition of the word *syad* (maybe) to every "truth" claim (117).

The story of the "The Elephant and the Blind Men" encapsulates this world view. The elephant is far more complex than any one of the men is able to experience. Therefore, each of their descriptions is based on their limited and idiosyncratic experience of the beast. Each one describes only one aspect of the elephant and it is only when they are taken together, in all their complexity and contradiction, that the animal in its entirety can in any way be known. The conflict raised by the disparities in description, would be avoided within the Jainist tradition, by the addition of a *syad*, which would be a recognition of the contingency and contextuality of each perspective.

Jain texts illustrate the contradictory nature of truth in all its complexity. Mahavira, the founder of Jainism, for example, is reputed in the Bhagavati Sutra to have said:

> *The world is ... eternal. It did not cease to exist at any time. It was and is and will be. It is constant, permanent, eternal, imperishable, indestructible, always existent. The world is ... non-eternal, for it becomes progressive after being regressive. And it becomes regressive after being progressive. The soul is eternal, for it did not cease to exist at any time. The soul is non-eternal. For it becomes animal after being a hellish creature, becomes man after becoming an animal, and it becomes a god after it becomes a man (122).*

For the Jain, perspective limits perception. Therefore, as in this text, objects like the world and the soul can be simultaneously eternal and non-eternal, depending on how they are perceived at the moment.

The Jain's (and indeed the Talmud's) view of the truth is far more complex than western relativism. Western relativism is built on a foundation of skepticism, which denies the ability of humanity to discern the truth. Therefore the relativist looks at all answers, seeing each as potentially partially true, but more importantly as also partially wrong, and therefore as a series of theses which will face antitheses and become new syntheses. To Jainist relativism, each truth is in a sense an absolute truth, contradictory views add new understandings of the object, without challenging the others.

The story of the elephant builds on this complex view of the nature of truth. Truths, rather than complete, are both relative and a matter of perception. Just as the blind man could see only one part of the elephant, to him that part exemplified the whole. So too, we perceive but one aspect of the truth, based on our idiosyncratic point of view. The challenge is not to jump to the conclusion that what we have found is the absolute and only truth that exemplifies reality. It is a truth (relatively) for example, that the elephant's leg is like a pillar. As in the story, this statement is only falsified when one assumes that the entirety of the elephant is like a pillar. The Jain tradition rejects this supposition and suggests that we must be open to a multitude of, perhaps, contradictory, "truths." Each vision of the 'truth', complementary or contradictory, is both important and correct.

In recent years the doctrines of multi-sidedness have been connected with *ahimsa* (non-violence), which is another central aspect of Jainist philosophy. *Ahimsa*, perhaps the most well known aspect of Jainism, is viewed within the tradition as absolute. This is encapsulated in vegetarianism, but even extends, for some Jains, to an avoidance of crushing insects and other animals as one walks, or even an eschewal of breathing in microbes through the use of a facemask. Today, a refusal to attack the views of others, and indeed to see even contradictions as "truths", are perceived as a form of intellectual *ahimsa* (119).

A Generalized Dialectic

The multi-faceted dialectical model, built on rabbinic and Jain traditions, adduced here is based on the belief that all truth is contingent and contextual, and that there are many (maybe an infinity of) possible "correct answers." A Golden Rule, or "Great Principal" may be right for one tradition, or even many. Even so, it may not be the essential message for all religious traditions. Even within a tradition, that which is considered essential may well change over time based on the needs and realities of adherents. Indeed, a multiplicity of idiosyncratic "correct answers" may even be found concurrently based on differing world views of adherents living in different contexts with differing contingencies. This model suggests that all these answers are indeed "truths," and that an acceptance of them allows us to understand the "other." It also suggests that the search for the "essential message" blinds us from seeing the "other" as he or she truly is, allowing us only to see them within our own contingent and contextual "correct answers."

This model also provides useful examples of a pluralistic approach towards peoples and traditions different than our own. Hillel's respect for Shammai's opinions, though they differed in every case from his own, and the Jainist use of intellectual *ahimsa* (non-violence) which demands a respect, indeed an acceptance of contradictory truths, provide a model very different from a world where our particular truths are most often viewed as the single "truth" to which all must conform.

Based on this model of dialectic, interfaith dialogue would therefore no longer be concerned with identifying the kernel of truth, "the essential message," which unites all religions. Nor would dialogue aim at the comfort of similarity, avoiding difficult issues, difference and distinction. Instead, it would aim to value and examine difference and diversity of the participants and traditions. It would demand an openness to hearing "truths" that are different than our own, without necessitating that we take them on, but asking that we be open to the realization that they also "truth" statements.

VI

Moving Away From Essential Messages

As has been shown, the meta-narrative (over arching narratives used to structure discourse) of religious essentialism – a search for the unifying basis that is common to all religion was one of the dominant narratives that shaped the discourse at the 1893 World's Parliament of Religions. Indeed, this narrative has continued to be influential to the present. It is built on the conception that all religions can be tied together in an essential way, and that the unity can be achieved by creating a focus on similarity and uniformity, rather than on difference and diversity. There are, however, serious challenges posed by the current modes of interaction built upon this narrative, as it has the potential to create blindness to authentic and important differences between traditions.

Initially, the narrative of "essential message" was not chosen intentionally to blind people to truths about the other traditions, rather it may have become the focus because of the fear that any controversy or extreme difference would prevent the formation of trust and sufficient comfort to overcome centuries of troubled relations. Advocates of unity built on the essential messages of religion perceived a troubled world, which was broken into diverse nations, and traditions, many of which were at odds with the others. Unifying humanity into a single religion was seen as a balm for the violence inherent in the world.

Subsequently, even though unity no longer is the explicit goal of interfaith efforts – it is seen as sufficient by most merely to identify the essentials that unite all religions – this approach also led to avoidance within interfaith dialogues and other programming of any subject, be it political or theological that could be seen as divisive or difficult for speakers or attendees. It also often led to the prevalence of large-scale presentations where "safe" speakers were chosen who could be trusted to represent their religions in a way that supported this narrative of essential similarity.[74]

---

[74] Dialogues often focus on peace, poverty, or other social justice issues where the general sentiments of presenters will be the same. It is rare for theo-

The choice we face today is to remain in this seemingly "safe" narrative or to move in a new direction, where difference and diversity are embraced and understood, rather than feared. Perhaps, therefore, the first question asked in the face of this choice is, 'why change when we have built positive relationships through the narrative of agreement – or essential message?' It is suggested here that these relationships are built on a false picture of the "other," where we see only ourselves – our values and ideas mirrored perforce through dialogues that focus only on similarities. True relationships, on the other hand, are built on seeing and accepting the other for what he or she truly is. Indeed the dialogues built on creating comfort may have been an important first step, but they are insufficient for the twenty-first century.

While it may be true that many of the world's religious traditions share some similarities, especially in the area of ethics and values, over emphasis on these similarities may blind us to a true understanding of other traditions. The Dalai Lama, for example, has been widely quoted as saying, "Every religion emphasizes human improvement, love, respect for others, sharing other people's suffering. On these lines every religion has more or less the same viewpoint and the same goal."[75] While it is difficult to argue with the values that underlie the quote, it is doubtful that all religious traditions were examined before this defining meta-narrative was created. Are all the approaches identical and would traditions that fail to embrace this message not be "authentic religions?"[76]

Such over-emphasis can imply that the "truths" which we identify out of our narrative of "essential message" are the essence of religion, while all the particularities within religious traditions are the "dross" to be discarded as the similarities alone are embraced. This result is a denial of idiosyncratic beliefs and rituals that the individual religions may see as the true essentials of their own traditions. Indeed, when taken together the identified essentials forming the meta-narrative are themselves often unsatisfying, as they are both too broad and too minimal to help anyone better understand any faith, let alone the diverse religious traditions from across the globe.

---

logical issues to be addressed, as these may be too divisive and can lead to serious controversy.

75   Widely attributed to the Dalai Lama, cited in Wikipedia: Ethic of Reciprocity and hundreds of other websites; source and date not cited. See, for example http://en.wikipedia.org/wiki/The_Golden_Rule

76   See below.

The religious essentialism narrative, however, is not only a failure in achieving understanding or unity it also can be dangerous. Identification of essentials is always an idiosyncratic process – as was demonstrated in the analysis of Hirsch and Higginson's presentations at the 1893 World's Parliament of Religions. They aimed at universality, but in the end all the essentials they identified were built on their own traditions. The narrative perforce seems to prioritize one particular faith tradition, or group of faith traditions attempting to shoehorn all the others into the same mold.

The narrative of religious essentialism served, perhaps, as a useful first step in the interfaith endeavor. It provided reassurance both for interfaith activists and for attendees at events, allowing them to identify comfortable similarities – be they about ethics, values, or very broad concepts of the divine – which enabled them to feel that they were on the road to finding the "truth" of religion, that all religions have an ultimate similarity and are together universal.

Through this process, however, activists became blind to the ultimate failure of the meta-narrative of religious essentialism. Dialogue and discussion while built on the demonstration of "sameness," pointed to difference and diversity.[77] As noted, these differences were ignored or dismissed as merely the dross, blinding us to an inner truth that was the same for all. This attempt at creating the grand narrative of religion, however, instead of leading to a better understanding of the world's diverse religions (and to creating an environment of better understanding and cooperation between people from differing traditions) has instead created a simulacrum of religion. We create whitewashed versions of our traditions, where each looks and sounds much like all the others. Our broad taxonomies, which gave us comfort, instead of helping us understand each other, have been masking the specific characteristics and individualities that make our religions what they are.

Indeed, meta-narratives and even taxonomies such as "religion,"[78] "movement," and "denomination" can be dangerous, as each also masks the

---

77 Scholarly analysis of the 1893 World's Parliament of Religions has suggested that this was the ultimate result of the event. While it aimed at establishing unity and universality, it was most successful in demonstrating plurality, locality and contextuality. See, for example, (Seager, 1993: 9),

78 Religion is a dangerous taxonomy because it is nearly impossible to define. Does, for example, a religion require a belief in a god, or need to have any creed of beliefs at all? When taken broadly it becomes essentially meaningless, while when defined more narrowly it can become a mirror of the culture of the defining party. The parameters of the definition define which traditions are seen an authentic "religion" and which traditions are out.

individual and can lead to misunderstandings and broadly conceived stereotypes. The identification of paradigm or *weltanschauung* is quite difficult to construe as it must take into account all the complexities of identity construction. An American or Canadian, for example, from any religious tradition may well have a different sense of his or her tradition than a person from the same religious tradition living in a more traditional society.

Even narratives such as the "family of religions," (a common theme of interfaith events) can be construed too narrowly (and therefore as exclusionary). It implies a genealogical connection, and a kinship based on a basic set of similarities that unite the entire "family" within the interfaith movement. This model would tend to exclude any tradition that does not enshrine or essentialize the "familial" similarities.

The interfaith movement utilizes a variety of narratives of universality or essentiality to create a level of comfort, thought necessary to enable interfaith cooperation, coexistence and perhaps ultimately unity. Yet, when these are examined critically not only are the "similarities" paper thin, but it also becomes clear that these narratives are a conscious or unconscious attempt to fit everything into a neat scholarly, political or particular religious mold. These unifying narratives abound in the interfaith world where it is not uncommon to hear about the Golden Rule, "People of the Book," and the "Abrahamic Faiths."[79] Each of these gives priority to a faith or group of faiths, defining all other religions within the context of the prioritized faith(s).

The "People of the Book" and "Abrahamic Faiths" narrative is particularly troubling, giving, as it does, priority and legitimacy to a small subset of religions. This narrative implies that only Judaism, Christianity and Islam are true religions because they all share the "God of Abraham," and in some way are all connected with the faith of that patriarch. This narrative is often imposed because of the fear – unfortunately often accurate – that one or more of the "Abrahamic" traditions will not participate in an interfaith event that includes polytheistic religions, which could be deemed as idolatrous, thus limiting the scope of multi-religious discourse.

The distinction between "Abrahamic" and "non-Abrahamic" was re-

---

79   The last two of these, "People of the Book" and "Abrahamic Faiths" are a reflection of the fact that interreligious discussions were largely between Jews, Christians and latterly Muslims until the end of the twentieth century. Their inclusion as meta-narratives does not challenge the fact that that there are historical connections between Judaism, Christianity and Islam, rather it suggests that these narratives tend to limit discussion to these three faiths.

cently brought home to me using slightly different terminology. A scholar, involved in the interreligious dialogue, suggested that I confused the terms interfaith and interreligious.

> *These are not interchangeable terms, as [D. Kunin] seems to think. Christian-Jewish dialogue, for example, is interreligious but not in any sense interfaith. We may be bound (religio) to the One God of Israel differently, but our Christian faith is in the One God of Israel. Hence Jewish-Christian dialogue is interreligious but not interfaith. We Christians know no other God than the God of Abraham and Sarah, though we may understand the One God of Israel a shade differently, though not incompatibly. So equating interfaith and interreligious is an error of fact.[80]*

For him, the term interreligious (deriving religion very narrowly – indeed based on a derivation that has been disputed since ancient times – from the Latin) includes only Jewish, Christian, and perhaps Muslim relations because these traditions serve the same God (and perhaps can be construed as the expression of the same religion). All other relationships were in these terms interfaith, because, presumably, their service is not oriented to the one "true" God. This narrative selects a limited definition of the divine as its essential message and as its defining factor of religion, and thus serves to exclude and indeed question the validity of the religious expressions of well over half the world's population. It also implies the equally troubling notion that Judaism and Christianity (and perhaps Islam) are in essence the same religion, an idea that would be problematic for most Jews if not for most Christians. I, therefore, choose to continue to use terms like interfaith and interreligious synonymously.

Other narratives exist, not as forms of exclusion, but rather in an attempt to redress long-standing injustices. One narrative of this type, "Indigenous Religion," groups together widely disparate traditions from all across the globe. It too does not, however, create an authentic understanding of these very diverse traditions. John A. Grim notes the com-

---

80 Quoted from an anonymous peer review of my article, "Multifaith: New Directions" (Kunin, 2013) sent to me on 13/10/11. For a discussion on the derivation of religion see Dubuisson's examination of the academic concept of religion, (Dubuisson, 2007: 788). The distinction between the Abrahamic and non-Abrahamic faiths is of long standing. Masuzawa also examines the derivation of the category and points to texts dating from the 17th to the 19th centuries where a version of the taxonomy first pertains (Masuzawa, 2005: 38-71, 145).

plexity of this narrative, grouping as it does 200 million people, with distinct societies, kinship systems and mythologies. Nonetheless he suggests that there are family characteristics, which unite them, such as spontaneous religious experiences, holistic connections with the environment, and ritual systems designed to instill collective memories (Grim, 1998). It is doubtful that these defining characteristics were shown to be universal among all the thousands of indigenous traditions. They are also generalizations, telling little or nothing about any of the particular cultures. The question could also be asked, if a particular indigenous religion did not contain one of these elements is it still indigenous, and if a differently categorized religion had all of them, would it actually be an indigenous religion? The narrative, therefore, may be useful to achieve political ends and force the world to take indigenous people seriously, but it fails to allow us to appreciate the diversity of religious expression.

The process of imposing narratives (especially grand narratives such as religious essentialism) has been shown to reflect the dominant/dominated dichotomy where dissenting voices, methodologies and paradigms are seen as illegitimate, passé or anti-intellectual (Wilson, 2008: 57-58). As noted, meta-narratives of this type ignore difference in an attempt to create universal definitions. These definitions most often reflect the ideology of the predominant culture, which implicitly or even explicitly sees its narrative as authentic, while all others are seen as inferior. Within multi-faith this can be seen in the attempt to find, or even to impose essentialist narratives, be they the Golden Rule (as shown, at root a very Jewish or Christian concept) or definitions of what qualifies as a religion, or basic definitions of spirituality on disparate traditions. More globally, and more insidiously, it can be seen in the attempt to impose a western capitalistic model on third-world economies. In each of these cases a dominant majority (at least in perceived power or influence), either Western or Western-Christian, seeks to impose its ideology and sense of self on the rest of the world.

Within the world of multi-faith the modernist process of imposing a Western model is not new. In nineteenth century Europe (and in some circles today), as was seen at both the Columbian Exposition and World's Parliament of Religions, Western culture and its religion, Christianity – in most cases Protestant – was viewed as the top of the social evolutionary tree, indeed it was the very goal of evolution (an interesting misreading of Darwin). When Western academics came to define terms like "religion," or "mysticism" Christian norms became the basis of the definitions (Dubuisson, 2007: 789).[81] So, for example, religion was defined in terms of belief (especially in a deity). Monotheism was deemed as the height of religious understanding. Daniel Dubuisson ironically notes, "human beings, whatever and wherever they may be, were supposed to reproduce in their behavior a type of which the archetype… most fully realized … would be found in the Christian West" (790). He also notes that even today religions are interpreted through the lens of Christianity, leading to either a rejection of the tradition as authentic, or to a disfigurement until they are "formatted to the Christian standard" (790). Indeed, the social-evolutionist approach, supported by the academic definition of religion, justified European colonizing and missionizing across the globe (and American and Canadian internal conquest and conversion of the native populations).

The misunderstandings of diverse traditions engendered by this meta-narrative of religion still persists today. Some question whether, based on the definition, Buddhism is a religion at all since many Buddhists do not profess a belief in a deity.[82] Others look with confusion at Judaism, as an example, since it is not a creedal religion. While Judaism has many beliefs, it is most often left to adherents to choose among them. There is no official creed (beyond a fairly abstract acceptance of monotheism), even Maimonides' famous "Articles of Faith" are not universally considered authoritative. Traditional Judaism is therefore more accurately seen as an orthopraxy (an authoritative set of practices), rather than an orthodoxy (an authoritative set of beliefs). These misunderstandings persist, even at interfaith events, where people often ask what the "official" Jewish belief is, or express surprise that Jews generally do not define or express themselves theologically.[83]

81 Dubuisson adduces the following as the Christian norms which became seen as the universal essentials of religion: faith in God, immortality of the soul, eternal life, contempt of the body and of the flesh. See also, p. 795.

82 See, for example, Masuzawa's discussion of the creation of Buddhism as a unified religion by Western academics in the nineteenth century (Masuzawa, 2005: 130). Many felt that Buddhism at its purist was a philosophy and not a religion – and therefore not a competitor with Christianity for the status of the world unifying religion.

83 Like the present author, Dubuisson rejects the idea that all religious share a basic essential message. He suggests that the narrative of essential message is based on "epistemological inheritances from theological monotheism in the operations of modern science" (Dubuisson, 2007: 790).

Meta-narratives have the power of exclusion, as their defining characteristics create artificially based barriers defining those who are in and those who are not. The narrative of the essential message of religion, based as it was and is on Western Christianity and views of social evolution, led to the exclusion in participation of any form of "primitive" or indigenous religion at the 1893 World's Parliament of Religions. There was a clear distinction drawn between religion and shamanism and fetishism. These "primitive" forms of religion were relics of the past and had no place at the table in the discussion of religion of the present (Dubuisson, 2007: 793). Whole categories of activities which did not fall within the parameters of the narrative, were labeled, for example as magic, and therefore outside the pale of "religion" (793). These narratives still largely pertain in scholarship today.[84]

While these meta-narratives persist in our modernist society, French post-modern thinker Jean-Francois Lyotard suggests that we are in a time of radical epistemological and ontological crisis, since it has become increasingly clear that the meta-narratives that academia (and in this case interfaith activists) created to organize society do not work (Bertens, 1993: 48).[85] He posits that they are so broad that the "other" is lost, and are an excuse to impose the majority on the minority. This is demonstrated, as is discussed elsewhere, by the similarities adduced by concepts such as the Golden Rule or other religious "essential messages." Not only are these are so general as to tell us little about the culture or world view of other traditions or people, but they also mask the other with their imposition of implicit Western biases. Indeed, they blind us to the realities and complexities of any tradition or traditions other than our own.

Lyotard's critique of modernism and all meta-narrative is reinforced by Zygmunt Bauman's examination of the social sciences, which could also be aimed at the interfaith world. He states, "They [meta-narratives] informed of contingency while believing themselves to narrate necessity, of particular locality while believing themselves to narrate universality" (Bauman, 1991: 232).[86] Bauman suggests that the social sciences aimed

---

84   These distinctions interestingly pertain in the study of Jewish Mysticism. Until recently theurgic mysticism (magic) was seen as less authentic (and therefore less worthy of study) than theosophical or prophetic Kabbalah.

85   Lyotard also suggests that meta-narratives obscure the "clouds of sociality," and therefore allow for increased power and efficiency by power structures. (Lyotard, 1993: 72).

86   Bauman also notes that truth claims solely arise in the context of hege-

at finding universal models and patterns in their interpretations of, for example, human society. Instead, they identified local and contingent (time-bound) factors necessary for understanding of those societies. Like the academic, interfaith activists who attempt to impose similarity and to identify "essential message" have also highlighted the idiosyncratic and diverse nature of world religions.

In relation to the modernist attempt to impose its narratives on our understanding of the world, Jacques Derrida suggests that there is a need for us to abandon all reference to a center, subject, or privileged reference, origin or an archia (Derrida, 1993: 232). The meta-narrative is a distortion of reality, reflecting a modernist "amnesia" – a refusal to see the world in all its complexity. He provides a historical critique of all meta-narratives, whatever their origin, isolating them within particular times, places, genders and classes. Every discourse, he notes, is *bricoleur* using the inter-textual meaning at hand to create and construct meaning (232). Like all aspects of human culture, the narratives that we construct in order to understand the world are all bound within both the time and power structure that created them. He demonstrates that the essentialist narratives, like the Golden Rule, which are used to create interfaith discourse are themselves contingent and contextual.

This rejection of meta-narratives of religious essentialism is complicated by the complexity of identity construction that renders each person as idiosyncratic. Noted anthropologist Levi-Strauss suggests a process of *bricolage* – a process of using cultural elements in one's surrounding – as a means whereby sets of signs – cultural objects (words, symbols or objects) – are invested with meaning. He suggested that the key aspect of the process of creating meaning is not based on a conscious selection of the best materials that might be used for the purpose, but rather is the unconscious adaption of materials that are on hand which fit into the underlying structure of the society (Levi-Strauss, 1966: 19). The material used may be recycled and reused again within the same society, or within different societies to express vastly different ideas. This interpretation reinforces the contingent nature of identity, as it is constructed unconsciously as each of us uses the materials found in our proximity.

While Levi-Strauss focused his concept of *bricolage* on the creation of mythological thought, others have also extended it to other societal

---

mony and proselytism (Bauman, 1991: 233).

expressions, such as rituals, religion or aspects of interpretation of material culture (Kunin, 2001: 52). For Levi-Strauss *bricolage* is an unconscious process, by which the cultural elements used for construction are unimportant, and only the underlying structural patterns that establish signification for the community are important, anthropologist Seth Kunin adds a degree of agency to the theory of *bricolage* through the concept of *jonglerie*, or the juggling of identity. "*Jonglerie* highlights the fact that to some extent individuals and groups consciously negotiate their sense of identity" (42). Kunin suggests that human identity is constructed of a variety of contested elements, which are constantly in a process of negotiation. At different moments of life there are both conscious and unconscious emphases on differing aspects of an individual's identity. Religious identity and self-definition will therefore also be in a constant state of negotiation by the elements that make up the individual (gender, class, religion, etc.), and also by his/her time and place.

This analysis of identity – whether religious or general – suggests the complexities through which it is constructed. It is not unlikely that people within one area, especially in a country as diverse as Canada or the United States, even people from the same general cultural or religious group, will have a multiplicity of world views with a wide variety of contested elements. Kunin's work suggests that it is only possible to create very general taxonomies (classifications) when creating narratives of group identity. There must, however, always be the recognition that the external and internal borders of these taxonomies are extremely malleable, fuzzy and local. This serves to undermine the usefulness of any essentialist narratives.

These theorists point to another complexity within the process of creating grand unifying narratives. Though each person, in the context of formal or informal interfaith discourse, may come from a particular religious tradition or culture, this is only one aspect of his/her *weltanschauung*. Derrida and the other theorists suggest that the creation of an individual's world view is complex, and under continuous construction (Vidal, 2008: 3).[87] Hence, even attempts to make authoritative statements about an individual's religious tradition will be idiosyncratic presentations shaped within the context of the complexity of the individual's *weltanschauung*.

---

87 Vidal notes that Leo Apostel (a major theorist in the study of *weltanschauung*) suggests a more personal construction, a *bricolage* built on ones culture and language, but also on ones context and experience.

This analysis would suggest that the interfaith movement should value the local, particular and tentative. The purpose for interfaith activities should be to see and understand the other, rather than to create grand narratives, which artificially attempt to bring everyone together, or to impose (or try to discover) the shared "essential message" of all religion. Real peace, coexistence and understanding will come only when we value the other without any interest in making (or seeing) them like ourselves. Dialogue and other interactions, therefore, would not be considered failures, but indeed successes, if differences were identified rather than commonalities. Each participant in an interfaith interaction is a spokesperson of the "other" (who or what ever that may be). The attempt to identify any concept of "essential truth" should have no relevance. Therefore, the proposed model of interfaith dialogue or relation, which will be discussed in detail in a later chapter, is neither about transformation, nor about finding a unified essence but instead is about understanding and respect of the differences that make us uniquely who we are.[88]

---

88 It may be noted that this model is also a meta-narrative, however, the narrative adduced here avoids imposition, and broad characterization.

VII

Learning to Dialogue for Difference

WHILE THE WORLD'S PARLIAMENT OF RELIGIONS MAY have marked the beginning of modern interfaith interaction, there had already been a long history of dialogue, often but not always adversarial. Jewish-Christian dialogue, for example, has its roots in patristic literature. Justin Martyr's (100-165 C.E.) *Dialogue with Trypho* purports to be a conversation between Justin and a Jew named Trypho, demonstrating the superiority of Christianity over Judaism. While the dialogue may or may not describe an actual conversation between Jew and Christian, it did serve to a great extent as a model for medieval "dialogues," in that its goal, like the medieval interactions, was to present a one-sided proof of the truth of Christianity.[89] These events were great showpieces for the church in its attempt to convert the Jews of Europe.

The tenth century Muslim world, however, provides an interesting exception to this adversarial and triumphalist approach, embracing at least the beginnings of a pluralistic narrative. Contemporaneous Egyptian Muslim historian al-Hum'aydi describes somewhat disparagingly an interreligious discussion that occurred in a *Kalam* academy in Baghdad.[90]

> *One of the Spanish theologians – Abu Omar Ahmad ibn Muhammad ibn Sadi – visited Baghdad ... [He] was asked if he had the opportunity of attending ... one of the assemblies of Kalam. Yes, he answered, I attended twice, but I refused to go there for a third time ... for this simple reason, which you will appreciate: At the first meeting there were present not only people of various (Islamic) sects, but also unbelievers, Magians [Zoroastrians], materialists, atheists, Jews and Christians, in short unbelievers of all kinds. Each group had its*

---

[89] Judah Halevi's *Kuzari* uses a similar literary device to prove the superiority of Judaism over philosophy, Christianity and Islam.

[90] *Kalam* a tenth century school of Muslim philosophy that was heavily influenced by ancient Greek thought.

> own leader, whose task it was to defend its views, and every time one of the leaders entered the room, his followers rose to their feet and remained standing until he took his seat. In the meanwhile, the hall had become overcrowded with people. One of the unbelievers rose and said to the assembly: we are meeting here for discussion. Its conditions are known to all. You, Muslims, are not allowed to argue from your books and prophetic tradition since we deny both. Everybody, therefore, has to limit himself to rational arguments. The whole assembly applauded these words…they proposed that I should attend another meeting in a different hall, but I found the same calamity there (Altman, 1969: 14-15).

While a modern pluralistic multi-faith dialogue would not, and should not, limit the use of any scripture in describing a particular faith, nor should it be a debate where one side or another attempts to score points in the establishment of truth. This ancient dialogue is unique in that all religious, and indeed non-religious, beliefs were permitted to present themselves on an equal footing. There is no indication, in this text, that the majority religion – Islam – was exerting its power (though this may have been an implicit hope), as was done in the Jewish-Christian dialogues of the Middle Ages, to encourage the conversions of the other minority participants. Like many modern dialogues, however, the pluralistic freedom expressed in this narrative is tempered by the idea that an essential single universal truth can be established through the discussions and debates.

Narratives of conformity and universality still form an important, implicit and often explicit, element with Western culture. Though, for example, in theory Americans and Canadians value individuality, there is also a constant pressure, from the media and other outlets, to act, speak and be more "American" or "Canadian." This, in extreme, leads to bigotry and xenophobia against perceived minorities. Within the interfaith movement this pressure for conformity is also exemplified by the desire, by many, to overemphasize the similarities rather than differences between faith groups.

While, the discovery of, and stress on, the similarities does create a degree of comfort which can enable differing communities to work in concert one with another, when it becomes the focus (or a perceived end instead of means) of interfaith discussion and dialogue then, as discussed earlier, it not only masks the unique aspects of varied religious traditions, but in truth creates an artificial unity where we see the other only through ourselves.

Indeed, our religious traditions are diverse, with vastly differing histories, understandings of the divine (or even if there is a divine), views of spirituality, and foci. Even religions like Judaism, Christianity and Islam,[91] which share a common thread of traditions and text, and claim relatively similar monotheistic view of the divine, are very different one from another. The idea of the Trinity, for example, would be considered antithetical to the monotheistic understandings of both Judaism and Islam. Even in cases where there are commonalities between various traditions, one religion may see a value as its Golden Rule, while another tradition might see that same value as merely one among many others. Indeed, the seemingly shared value might mean a very different thing when it is placed into its context within another religious tradition.

The search for commonality, therefore, should be only the beginning of dialogue rather than its conclusion. The comfort it creates should be built on an explicit goal that it merely is there to provide a firm foundation to begin the far more difficult and dangerous process of appreciating and understanding the differences among communities and traditions, that is to say, real interfaith communication and understanding. If commonality is the desired conclusion rather than just the start, then perhaps no true dialogue has occurred.

Dialogue, or even the simplest communication, among people of faith – and of no faith – is essential to create bridges of understanding and acceptance. It is the keystone, which enables us to learn about other traditions and to educate others about our own. Every moment when we meet another human being is an opportunity for formal and informal dialogue. Yet dialogue (whether formal or informal) is easier as a dream or ideal, than its actualization in reality. Unlike summit meetings and peace conferences where an outside force uses its greater power to bring hostile parties together and to force a resolution, true interfaith dialogue can only occur when there is a sense of equality and comfort for all, when there is a feeling of mutuality and a like-minded commitment to learn and to build understanding.

---

91   There are many sects, approaches and denominations within each of these traditions. Their views may also vary widely on many issues, adding to the complexity of interaction. In many cases, as noted above, internal differences may often create more difficulties for intra-faith communications than external ones.

Indeed dialogue should also not only be seen as the big one time event staged between religious leaders and thinkers. Rather, true dialogue can take place at any time when people from differing or even the same traditions come together, be it for formal discussions or at more intimate informal social gatherings. A discussion around a table at a dinner or at a coffee house is as true and important a dialogue as one staged at a university. Indeed these informal opportunities may be of even greater importance because they can lead to the creation of ongoing relationships both between individuals and communities. In the Jewish tradition, for example, every meal can be seen as the locus of the presence of God when people come together with the desire to understand each other and to create peaceful coexistence.

The equality and respect, expressed so fully in the text describing multi-faith interaction at the *Kalam* academy, was to a degree missing (as was discussed in Chapter 1) at the 1893 World's Parliament of Religions, yet, it is the most essential element of successful and effective dialogue. Some have suggested that true dialogue requires at times a radical transformation in the theologies of the participants, in so far as it necessitates an acceptance of the legitimacy and "truth" of the other (Bayfield1992: 24-25). While this is indeed desirable, I would suggest that it is not an absolute requirement. Dialogue should not be predicated on agreement or even acceptance, rather it should be predicated on the willingness of all participants to listen and learn about the "other."

Dialogue provides an opportunity for sharing and for growth by all its participants. Unlike an argument or debate, its goal should be not to change beliefs or to convince the participants of the strength of one point of view and the weakness of the other. Rather, Leonard Swindler suggests that "dialogue is a two-way [or more] communication between persons who hold significantly differing views on a subject, with the purpose of learning more truth about the subject from the other" (Swindler, 2008: 11). While I would question Swindler's use of "truth," (as it might imply that there is a uniting "truth" that can be found beyond all individual religions) it is through this mode of communication that we begin to see the other as they would be seen and understood, thus dispelling both ignorance and preconceived notions. Indeed, Rabbi Tony Bayfield describes dialogue as most successful when it "acknowledges the worth of … independent faiths, permitting their exponents to be themselves" (Bayfield: 24). While Bayfield's work only addresses Jewish-Christian dialogue, his ideas are more broadly applicable. He, to my mind rightly, suggests that differing religions are like "apples and oranges," unique and unrepeatable (27).

S. Wesley Ariarajah describes dialogue as providing an opportunity to build a "community of conversation...where people learn to see differences among them not as threatening but as "natural" and "normal." He suggests that dialogue has the potential to create the relationships necessary to solve conflict not necessarily in the short but rather in the long term (Ariarajah, 1999: 14-21). He reinforces the idea that true dialogue cannot ignore or paper over difference, or even those areas that lead to conflict. Rather, it demands that we examine and discuss exactly those issues. It is only when we dispel misconceptions, ignorance and stereotypes and gain instead an informed perspective of other peoples' experiences embracing difference and diversity that we can create a vibrant community of peoples.

This opportunity presented by dialogue, to shed misconceptions and stereotypes, is unfortunately often missed. People get caught up in the self-satisfaction of similarity and fail to move beyond these comforting thoughts to the more challenging discussions about real differences. We celebrate as "fact" the misconception that every religion has its version of the Golden Rule, and miss the point that it is our differences that to a great extent define us. Religions – cultures – are not all identical (with only minor external variances), and it is only when we face these differences that we can begin to see and understand both the "other" and ourselves.

True communication and the creation of relationship are therefore also impeded because of the failure in most of our organized dialogues to confront the critical issues that separate people of faith. Instead of examining the hard issues that separate different religions, we choose topics where everyone can speak in generalities demonstrating how wonderful and benevolent their traditions are, while ignoring the elephant, that is to say the all-too real conflicts that might create tension or disrupt feelings of fellowship. The most common topics for dialogues, therefore, are social issues such as peace, poverty or the environment, where all participants are drawn from a relatively similar secular environment and express views that, while drawn from their traditions, are relatively the same. Yet if the more difficult issues were faced, frank discussion could create true understanding and effect real change in attitudes.

The failure of our formal dialogues, as we shy away from complex issues, is demonstrated by the questioning that often follows the presentations. Listeners are rarely satisfied with the generalities, litanies of similarities and self-satisfaction expressed. The questions they ask often bring up the very areas of concern, which both planners and presenters have attempted to avoid. These are often phrased in angry or hostile terms, attacking some or even all of the represented traditions. This anger may, in part, be engendered because of the attempt by the speakers to paper over the real challenges and conflicts that exist.

Unfortunately, even in the rare cases where difficult issues are discussed, differences and challenges are glossed over as each presenter attempts to situate his tradition with the "desired" uniform message. A recent dialogue of religious views on gender minorities, held at the University of Alberta, demonstrates this failure. Each participant, from diverse global religions[92], suggested that, aside from a radical fringe, their traditions were open and accepting, or at least loving, towards the gender-differenced community. This, and not more conservative positions, was they claimed the "essential message" of religion. As was just discussed, it was left to members of the audience to question and challenge the narrative thus presented, as they reflected on their personal and community experiences, most especially their feelings of rejection, when approaching the represented traditions.

While there is truth to the fear that controversial opinions may alienate attendees who also desire an "essential message" that mirrors their own beliefs, and who don't want to hear voices, especially from their "own" traditions, that confront their narratives. It is just these challenges that make dialogue meaningful. One interfaith event on parenting was deemed as a failure by its organizers when a conservative Christian presenter's point of view was very troubling to the more liberal Christian attendees. The true failure here, not perceived by the organizers, was the unwillingness of the attendees to hear a voice (relatively from their own tradition) that did not mirror their own views.[93]

---

92 Participants included a Jew, two Buddhists, a Muslim, two Christians (from the United Church of Canada, and the Pentecostal Church) and an atheist.

93 Interestingly, in this case it was clear that they would not have had a problem hearing the same views from a presenter from another faith. Often, intra-faith relations (because we embrace the false idea that the same narratives should be shared) are more complex than multi-faith relations.

As has been discussed, a focus on the differences between traditions has the potential to be both dangerous and divisive. Indeed, people entrenched in their own belief systems may be horrified by beliefs and traditions far different than their own. So, for example, strict monotheist may be shocked on seeing or hearing about the multiple images of gods found in a Hindu temple. Yet, the future of interfaith understanding and positive relationships requires that we approach other faiths (and indeed our own faith) with an openness, not to change our own belief systems, but rather with a desire to learn about other world faith expressions without judgment.[94]

Dialogue, in this sense is not predicated on transformation of one's tradition, or theology. Indeed, there is no call for one to abandon oneself to be part of the process. Rather, the opposite is true; a dialogue is most successful when each participant openly and honestly shares who he or she is and what he or she believes. Yet, there are two levels of transformation (beyond a greater understanding of another's perspective) that implicitly occur. The first level is the transformation of knowledge of self. Self-revelation built on introspection and self-acceptance is a necessary prerequisite of speaking with integrity and authenticity. The second level is also introspective in that it demands a confrontation with one's own prejudices, fears and hatreds, rather than on those of the other participants. On both of these levels self-understanding along with greater understanding of the other, is the desired transformative end of dialogue.

An added complexity to interfaith understanding is the idiosyncratic nature of interfaith presentations, created by the ongoing development of religious traditions and the complexity of identity construction. Religion like any other aspect of human culture is constantly changing and developing as it responds to the realities faced by adherents. In addition, each

---

94 This can be problematic when another faith, or culture, embraces something that falls outside our ethical norms. There are times when serious and dangerous differences arise, as in the case of female genital mutilation or honor killing, to list but two. In these situations the life and health of others is at risk, and I would suggest that we have a right both to speak out and reach out demanding that these practices be abandoned. There are also times when our modern western narratives are challenged. In these cases, such as distinctions between genders, we should be careful not to view our values as absolute. There are also gray areas where care is needed. Male circumcision, for example, is an important ritual in Judaism and Islam. While many view it as unnecessary surgery, there is also significant research suggesting, in some cases significant health benefits.

person also, perforce, can bring only their own unique understanding of their tradition; an understanding shaped by their personal history and world view. One presenter might understand the differing roles of women in some traditional forms of Judaism as sexist while another might stress the differing spirituality of one gender as compared to another. Indeed, such explanations are not static, but develop overtime as human culture changes and evolves.

These complexities render all interfaith presentations and dialogues as idiosyncratic, local and contingent. Yet, even so they still remain the essence of interreligious understanding. Listening and participating in dialogue, for example, enables us to begin to understand something of the "other," as we allow them also to understand something of ourselves. At its best dialogue helps us to understand the uniqueness of each human being, and the diversity of expression even within a single faith group or culture. Rather than creating narratives, which artificially attempt to bring everyone together, or to impose (or try to discover) the shared "essential message" of all religion, real peace, coexistence and understanding will come only when we value the other without any interest in making (or seeing) them like ourselves.

It has been posited that there are three preconditions which are necessary for successful dialogue: an openness to learn from the other; knowledge of one's own traditions, and an equally knowledgeable partner (Swindler: 12). While at least the first of these conditions is important, I suggest that the second condition needs to be nuanced or reconsidered. The second condition implies that deep knowledge is important for dialogue. While this may be true for large scale staged events, where the education of the attendees is as important as the creation of relationships, yet even scholars and religious leaders can learn equally from simple adherents of another tradition as from another scholar. Deep knowledge should not be a requirement for communication or the creation of relationship.

There is another, more fundamental challenge to successful dialogue in addition to these previously discussed. The human mind works through the imposition of systems. We take in stimuli, whatever the source be it tactile, verbal, or visual, and we use internal systems to fit them into a structure of understanding. Philosopher and theologian Peter Rollins suggests, "we never see the world as it really is…but always place meaning onto it" (Rollins. 2008: 10). This level of interpretation creates a barrier between the other and ourselves. Buber, therefore, suggests that content-less dialogue is the meeting place of the "I" and the "Thou" (the you) (Buber, 1970: 59). Indeed, Buber identifies the true moment of dialogue as a place where "the relation to the You is unmediated. Nothing conceptual intervenes between the I and the You" (62). Without content, he implies, we allow for a true encounter with the other without the imposition of self or ego. These authentic moments of dialogue are infinitesimally short, he contends, because we, perhaps perforce, almost immediately begin to add content and therefore turn the other into an object, an "it" rather than a "you (63). Buber points here to the challenge in all communication, as we listen we interpret and begin to see the other in our own terms, rather than in his or her own. This challenge is especially germane in interfaith dialogue where unfamiliar traditions are presented, as it is a normal human reaction to attempt to normalize the unfamiliar "other" by placing it within an accepted model or narrative.

Buber points out that humanity generally sees the world and all that is in it in a utilitarian way. Everything (even another person) is examined within the context of how it (he or she) is useful. In this way we transform and see all things and people as objects, or in Buber's terms "it," rather than as a "you;" something we can enter into a relationship with. Dialogue, as an "I" and "Thou" process, then, is primarily about the creation of relationship and not about enhancing communication or understanding. There is almost a mystical sense that it is the realization underlying connectivity of all being that is the basis of Buber's concept of dialogue. True dialogue, in this sense, reveals a connectivity and relationship not only between one human and another and between one human and the world, but also more fundamentally between humanity and the divine.

While Buber is certainly correct in identifying this challenge to ongoing, content-rich dialogue, is it sufficient to curtail all but the briefest silent encounters? It could rather be suggested that Buber's silent content-less dialogue is only the necessary first step to true dialogue, as the participants first realize the "I"-"Thou" relationship. If we stop here, however, we are still trapped in our perceptions, because we immediately begin the unconscious process of interpretation and objectification as we place that person (or thing) within a narrative or existing taxonomies. Perhaps, instead, the next stage of authentic dialogue should be the time of listening, without – as much as possible – interpretation. Or, at the very least listening with the realization that what we hear and understand has been interpreted through our internal cognitive systems. We need to open ourselves to hear what the other person is telling us, without trying to compare or contrast or fit it into preconceived models – when we interpret we objectify the "other." Through this process, the relationship built by the silent Buberian dialogue, is enhanced as we come to appreciate not only the unity but also the diversity of all that exists.

Once dialogue moves beyond silence to content, objectifying of the other can also take the form of judgment and attempts to discern truth. As we listen to the other it is difficult not to explicitly or implicitly judge their "truths" based on our own.[95] We create criteria, generally areas where our tradition excels, and examine the other based on these. Or, we take criteria, which are normative from our secular world view (gender roles, are one example) and use these to judge other traditions. This process is an internal mirror of the search for "essential messages" built on a hierarchy of traditions, which perforce prioritizes our own. Through this process of comparison, judgment and attempted discernment of truth we not only objectify the other, but we also lose them in ourselves.

The complexity of this process is demonstrated in the influential work on interfaith dialogue of twentieth century Catholic theologian Raimon Panikkar (Panikkar, 1999). Panikkar also notes the challenge and limitations of the Buberian content-less dialogue, as being insufficient as a means of creating understanding and appreciation. Like Buber he suggests that the first essential meeting is between the "I" and "Thou" – an experience of the connection between humans, or between humanity and God. Unlike Buber, however, he suggests that this meeting is only the beginning of authentic dialogue, which he believes is a transformative process. The next step he contends, based on the Golden Rule, is a true love and acceptance, indeed the embrace of the other's belief (Panikkar: 48-51). For Panikkar, true dialogue not only challenges a person, but it must also change him or her. One who engages in dialogue, he suggests, must be even be ready to convert if impelled by the experience (51).[96]

---

95 See, for example, (Cornille, 2009). Criteria of discerning the truth are presented from the perspectives if Judaism, Christianity, Islam, Buddhism, and Hinduism.

96 Interestingly, as noted above, Herman Melville in Moby Dick already suggested Panikkar's understanding that the Golden Rule impels him to accept the truth of the other as his own. Ishmael, when invited by Queequeg to a pagan ceremony, suggests that just as he would like Queequeg to become a Presbyterian,

Despite, however, this apparent openness to the other, and the expressed willingness to hear and be transformed by differing voices, Panikkar still imposes a structure (a series of lenses through which he views the other), based on his own tradition, upon his understanding of the "thou". He suggests, for example that "Christ is the Lord, but the Lord is neither only Jesus nor does my understanding exhaust the meaning of the word" (70). Or more tellingly, "Christ is the only mediator…he is present and effective in any authentic religion…Christ is the symbol, which Christians call by this name, of the ever-transcending but equally ever-humanly immanent Mystery" (70). These modes of interpretation force any observed religion into a Christian interpretive model of the meaning of faith, even if they actually work and understand the world in very different ways.

It may be difficult or even impossible to remove such lenses and not interpret the "thou" within a system of the "I". Yet, dialogue in which we actually experience the "thou" in his or her authenticity requires at least an attempt. It is here that the alternative Jain/Rabbinic dialectic, suggested earlier, is most important. When we hear, see or meet someone or something we immediately begin the process of judgment and categorization. With the traditional model of dialectic, and indeed even in Panikkar's non-dialectical approach to dialogue, we are also in the process of seeking the truth. Therefore, within the encounter of dialogue we also judge each new piece of knowledge within the context of a single truth. If something challenges – is an antithesis – of a previously held notion, is the challenge true, demanding transformation, or is it false and should be rejected? Either way a single synthesis is demanded.

In the new model of the dialectic of dialogue, which posits a multiplicity of truths, we move away from both "objectifying" and judging that which we hear or learn. Our egos should not be challenged or indeed gratified by what we find. Instead, we should listen with the interest built on the desire to hear and learn about another human within his or her own terms. The knowledge enriches us, even if it doesn't change us. We are, therefore, not troubled if their views or values challenge our own, since we are not seeking a single synthesis, the universal, but rather another of many truths.

One of the great challenges facing the interfaith movement has been its failure to engage with the conservative or more traditional elements within most religions. When the topic is brought up, the likely response is that these groups are not interested in dialogue, but instead are caught

---

so to the Golden Rule impels him (Ishmael) to become a pagan. (Melville: 54).

up in their own narratives, which claim possession of the "absolute truth." It sometimes appears that we are afraid to hear these voices, stemming from our own traditions – broadly construed – that are so different from our own.

It has recently been suggested (Frew, 2011) that these conservative traditions, especially Christian, have not been present because they are concerned about the goals of the interfaith movement. They fear a push to create a universal new syncretic religion.[97] This fear is reinforced by the emphasis on similarity so often proclaimed at interfaith events. It is also supported by the strong unity narrative present in the 1893 World's Parliament of Religions, and by unity ministries that claim to embrace all religions.[98] The concept of a single world religion fits in some conservative Christian's apocalyptical vision of the end times where such a syncretistic world unifying religion can be identified with the anti-Christ. This creates a level of suspicion and a refusal for engagement. I would suggest that there is also a concern that the goal of dialogue is transformation of the other, rather than an opportunity for learning and understanding.

The model of dialogue suggested here, with its open-ended dialectic, can answer both of these concerns. The dialectic built on a view of a multiplicity of discreet truths does not demand or even encourage change when a new truth is presented. All it demands is a willingness to listen and learn about the "other." The requirement for acceptance of that truth is not present. There is also no suggestion that one should gather all the truths to create something new. Indeed, this would be impossible as there is a likelihood that there would be a multiplicity of contradictory truths. This model of dialectic can make room for a multiplicity of voices in the world of multi-faith, be they conservative, atheist, agnostic or spiritual (but not religious) who have not been present in the past.

There often is also confusion between dialogue and debate. While dialogue aims at allowing all voices to be heard and valued leading to understanding, debate is concerned with scoring points and convincing the audience, and perhaps the opposing speakers, of the correctness of one's point of view. This confusion has led to a diffidence mitigating against or limiting participation on the part of some religious traditions. Orthodox Jewish leaders, for example, have often been suspicious of dialogue (most

---

97 See Chapter Six, "Narratives of Interfaith."

98 See, for example, the web site of the New Seminary, which trains interfaith ministers to work with people of all faiths. www.newseminary.org.

notably with Christians), expressing a fear that its ultimate aim is either conversion, or (as examined above) an attempt to create a syncretistic mix of diverse traditions.[99] To prevent such an outcome, a long list of forbidden subjects was created, severely limiting the possibility of dialogue leading to an understanding of the differing religious traditions.

This confusion has, in my experience, been amplified in recent years as new non-traditional (in the context of the interfaith dialogue) voices have come to be heard. Since the publication of Dawkins' *God Delusion* (2006) and Hitchen's *God is Not Great* (2007), atheists and agnostics have become important new voices in dialogue. Secular belief systems are a welcome new addition to the discourse, yet they, perhaps even more than representatives of religious faiths because of their scientific modernist and positivist approach, are committed to the Hegelian dialectic. At present their participation tends to transform dialogue into debate, as they attempt to score points by showing the absurdity of belief systems other than their own.[100] Indeed, it often seems that they are arguing against a caricature of religion (as do Hitchens and Dawkens) and a self-constructed straw man rather then the other voices present at the event.[101] Their presence, however, in dialogue will become most valuable when they gain the self-confidence to present their views without defining themselves against other systems and paradigms.

Indeed, opening dialogue to non-traditional voices, such as the atheist, agnostic, secular and new expressions of spirituality will be an important opportunity and challenge in the coming years as young people look for answers outside the boundaries of both the established faiths and the purely secular. Indeed, belief systems are not limited to the "religious," we all create or utilize systems of belief (whether in science, a deity, or something else) which allows us to function and understand the world.

---

99 See, for example, Soloveitchik, 2012.
100 I have seen this first hand in a number of dialogues, which have included representatives from atheist groups. At one event focusing on the existence of God, held at the University of Alberta in 2009, the atheist presentation focused on the proofs, which he said the Christian and Jewish speakers had used, even though neither spent any time trying to prove that God existed.
101 Hitchens for example, creates a straw-man version of religion based largely on Christian fundamentalism. His book also largely ignores eastern and new religions, and focuses mainly on Christianity, Judaism and Islam (Hitchens, 2007: 21-36).

Neil Gillman's analysis of the role of mythological thought in *The Death of Death* places these systems into the context of mythological thinking, adding a level of contingency (Gillman, 1997: 29). Gillman posits that myths form the spectacles through which we as humans interpret the world around us. They form a foundation through which we understand our relation to the world, to the rest of humanity and to the divine (itself a mythological construct). "A living myth works effectively on behalf of the members of a community. It gives meaning to their corporate lives" (27). Gillman suggests that the "truth" of these mythological structures is relative. They are "true" because they form the underlying foundation of a culture and cement identity, they create a structure by which we understand reality, and they are existentially true – they invoke responses within us, and because they allow us to live a meaningful integrated life. Mythological systems (even scientific systems) do not express "absolute truths," but rather are contingent and contextual. Any system, which provides spectacles through which humans understand the world, can be understood as a mythological system. The presence of voices of diverse older and newer structuring systems can only enhance the discourse of dialogue.

VIII

Narratives of Prayer

THE UNIFORMLY CHRISTIAN NATURE OF PUBLIC PRAYER AT the 1893 World's Parliament of Religions strongly shaped the dominant Christian inclusivism narrative of the event. Yet, in addition to dialogue, home observance, public ritual and prayer can be further bridges that help us to learn about one another. It is through prayer and ritual that we can often see beyond the cognitive to the emotional, the mystical and the spiritual. They help us to move beyond logical conceptualization to actual practice and experience of our own and likewise other traditions.

The truest way to experience other traditions is through participant observation, that is by attending, watching and participating to a level that is both comfortable for you and for the people whose ritual or worship you are observing. This can, however, produce significant challenges. Objectivity, in this case, is only the first challenge to be surmounted, others, such as comfort or even lack of conformity with one's own tradition may be even more difficult to overcome.

Like true dialogue , a successful participant observation requires objectivity. It requires a realization that one is not present to judge or even to compare, but rather to experience the other tradition within its own terms. While it is true that there can be commonalities in expression between some religious traditions, both in the forms of prayer and in ritual, if we seek them out we both blind ourselves to particularities and we impose our own self-constructed (or academic or societally-constructed) definitions and expectations on the other tradition. A prayer or ritual that appears similar may in truth play a very different role in diverse religions. Dwelling on commonalities is an expression of the narrative of "essential message." It constitutes a move from objectivity to ethnocentrism.

The impulse to judge, while observing prayer or ritual of (or indeed cognitively learning about) another tradition or even the different varieties within our own, arises when observed traditions seem to contradict values found in our Western culture, which we deem to be of ultimate importance. Many religions maintain, for example, age-old gender distinctions, which when interpreted from outside appear as a form of misogyny, or at very least appear to place women in a significantly subordinate role in the particular society. While sexism is certainly rife in the world, within the context of interfaith understanding, it is important both not to judge but also not to jump to conclusions. It is important to remember that one may be observing a culture, very different from one's own, with both different expectations and understandings of the world. So, for example, within traditional Judaism, a religion that maintains strong distinctions in religious roles for men and women, superior spirituality is the most common explanation for the exclusion of women from full participation in public worship. Traditional Orthodox women and men commonly accept this distinction. While Marx might call this an example of false consciousness, from an interfaith and multicultural perspective we must resist this narrative, and accept the perceptions of people as they wish to be understood.

Indeed, cultural and religious differences can often lead us to misjudge or misunderstand the motivations of other people. It is, for example, considered disrespectful or presumptuous, in many Asian countries for a young person, or a person of lesser status to look directly into the eyes of someone considered more senior. To many Westerners, however, the lack of direct eye contact may suggest dishonesty. Sexual norms, as a second example, may be vastly different from one culture, religion or tradition to another. In one society public kissing may be an appropriate, and in many cases, non sexual greeting, while in others it may be seen in much more intimate terms. Even touch between genders can be interpreted in diverse ways. In one culture a gesture like shaking hands may be seen as an essential demonstration of respect, while in another any physical contact between non-married men and women could be seen as a form of sexuality.

Traditional clothing (usually associated with diverse religions as diverse as Islam, ultra-Orthodox Judaism, and even forms of Christianity, e.g. the Amish) has also been seen as problematic by mainstream western society as it perceives people from outside the norm. This has led, perhaps because of Islamophobia, to a fear and even in some cases attempts (both in Europe and in Quebec) to legislate against the *hijab* and *berka*, garments utilized by traditional Muslim women. In an interesting backlash, some more Americanized Muslim women have taken on the *hijab* as a sign of their religious and cultural identity.

Particularistic beliefs and wordings of prayer may also be challenging to observers of traditions different from their own. Concepts such as "chosen people" in Judaism, the belief in many forms of Christianity that prayers only reach the Father (God) through the Son (Jesus), or that salvation is solely through belief in Jesus, are found in many different traditions. It is important to remember that during an observed ritual or service these are taken out of a much more complex theological structure, which may interpret them ways that are different than those assumed by the observer. There may well also be other trends within the particular religion, expressing other views, which are not reflected in the service or ritual. These beliefs, prayers or rituals also reflect a level of authenticity that is the object of participant observation. Interfaith interaction, as noted, does not require an acceptance of another tradition's belief, but rather a willingness to learn and to communicate without judgment. In all these cases, as in many others, context and the realization of diverse world views is essential to avoid misunderstanding and premature judgment of religions and traditions that evidence different values than our own.

Visiting a worship service, and participant observation, within the context of multi-faith requires respect but may in some cases not require (or even allow for) full participation. It is common courtesy to stand and sit (if that is requested)[102] in the same manner as the adherents of the tradition. It is also proper to recite the prayers, if one feels comfortable with the message and the language (sometimes the prayers will not be in English, and will therefore preclude participation). There may, however be prayers, which express a theology that may be uncomfortable, or represent particularistic traditions. In these cases, listening respectfully is always acceptable and appreciated. There often are, however, aspects of ritual that are open only to members of the particular faith or tradition. Thus, for example, the taking of a communion at a Catholic service is only appropriate if one is of that particular faith.

Prayer not only plays an important role in individual religious traditions, but also within civil society and the broader interfaith movement. When, however, joint prayer is planned, complex motivations and emotions lead to the embrace of a variety of narratives, which largely shape these events. These narratives reflect the broader goals that people bring to interfaith interactions.

---

102 In many cases all that will be expected is respectful sitting while those of the tradition may be kneeling or bowing as they observe the proper forms of their rituals or prayers.

The most common form of joint interfaith prayer is marked by an adherence both to political correctness and to the narrative of "essential message." At such events, be they sponsored by interfaith organizations or by various civic (or governmental, e.g. a mayor's prayer breakfast) groups, the prayers offered by religious leaders (lay or clergy) are generic and most often in English. Anything particular or difficult is avoided in order to assure the comfort of all the attendees. Thus, for example, the phrase "through Jesus Christ our Lord," is often omitted from Christian prayers, though it is an essential element in some Christian belief systems. Authenticity is sacrificed for the perceived comfort of the non-Christian participants in the event. The exclusion of the particular strengthens the narrative that ultimately we are all the same, at the cost of experiencing the realities of any of the participant traditions. [103]

The use of Jesus's name in a prayer, the expression of anything but very generic ethical sentiments, or chanting in a foreign language can only be perceived as problematic if we expect everyone to believe, think, act and pray in exactly the same way that we do. The expectations drawn from this narrative force all the participants to accept and conform to the norms of the generic universalist mainly secular majority. The authentic, on the other hand, challenges complacency and the narrative of "essential message." It represents a demand that we reexamine our fear of difference and embrace the fact of the diversity of human experience and expression.

Since the twentieth century, especially among younger people, particular religious identity has been weakened in favor of a more generic idea and syncretistic view of spirituality, encouraging experimentation and drawing belief and practice from diverse traditions, both religious and secular, to create their own idiosyncratic "religion". Others have worked to create new modern universalist ministries which they present as "interfaith." They collect or anthologize prayers, rituals and beliefs in what amounts to new religions. In many cases they claim the authenticity of all the traditions from which they drew, and may even perform specific rituals and ordain clergy for the more particularistic traditions.[104]

---

103 It could be argued that prayer breakfasts and Thanksgiving services are geared for communal cohesion, and therefore do not require a real experience of the other. I, however, would contend that these might provide the only chance of such an authentic experience on the part of many of the participants. It is therefore essential that the opportunity for education should not be missed.

104 This process is not new. Most religions are built on the structure of

This leads to interfaith services where prayers and rituals from a variety of traditions are removed from their original understandings and contexts and placed into new ones.

These new conglomerate belief systems represent an authenticity of their own, but they can be seen as problematic if viewed as an expression or goal of the broader multi-faith movement. When viewed this way, they are an expression of the narrative of uniformity and "essential message," and they implicitly deny the legitimacy of the more particularistic traditions. The Golden Rule, movement with its stress on the universality of this ethic, and its claim to be a "balm for overly theological religious consciousness" (Wattles: 85) represents just such a challenge to the legitimacy of the diversity of religious expression. A recent film, *Globalized Soul*, also exemplifies this narrative. The film focuses largely on Jainism and Islam with tangential mentions of Christianity and Judaism. It makes the dramatic claim that the various spiritual messages of the great world religions gathered together not only could heal the darkness of the soul, but also the social ills facing the world. Such goals take the spirituality out of the context of much broader and complex traditions and places them into a new and modern context. This new context does not represent continuity from the parent tradition, but rather something new and unique, whether or not the underlying transformation of the world can be achieved. Such movements are important modern phenomena, but they should not be the goal of multi-faith, which values the diversity of religious traditions, including these, and therefore does not aim at creating a uniform universal world religion.

During the last few years another form of joint interfaith prayer based on the narrative of acceptance of diversity has come to the fore. Discrete and authentic prayers from a multiplicity of individuals exemplify these multi-faith events. Rather than the similar, unparticular and English prayers that were the norm in the original interfaith services,

---

previous and contemporaneous traditions. Biblical myth, for example, is both created from and a response to those of Mesopotamia. Today, through the creation of "interfaith" and universalist traditions, the process is more self-conscious with much less distinction and barriers. So, for example, I was informed by a clergy member from one of these new traditions that she performed "Jewish" and "Catholic" weddings in the same weekend. Neither tradition was her own. I would suggest that her tradition was authentic in its own terms, but that the weddings she performed contained Jewish and Catholic elements, rather than representing authentic weddings from those religious traditions.

prayers in these events are done in an authentic way and most often in their original language, and where appropriate chanted. It is not uncommon at an interfaith event of this type to hear first-nation drumming, followed by a chant from the Qur'an and the intonation of "Hu" the Eckankar holy syllable. The narrative of commonality stressed in the these services is very diffuse, merely, perhaps, a common goal among religions to reach out beyond ourselves in something, that in a very general way, could be called prayer. It is, however, distinctiveness of mode, rather than similarity that is stressed.

These services require openness to the other and an acceptance of the particular. Prayers reflect unique theologies and beliefs, the challenge is to be open when they are built on concepts not our own. Instead of being offended, as in the case of non-Christians and especially Jews, when a Christian prays in Jesus' name, there needs to be a realization that this coda reflects an important aspect of Christianity, and indeed that for many the prayer would be meaningless without it. We get caught, I believe, in a trap built by a long history of negative interaction and perhaps ongoing Christian evangelization. Real acceptance, however, requires moving beyond the visceral reaction and stereotype to the realization and acceptance of difference in expression. The prayer with the coda is offered not to offend, but rather with the sincere hope for acceptance by God.

Multi-faith events, especially where authentic and particular prayers are offered, require the willingness to leave one's zone of comfort. This is especially true of adherents of monotheistic traditions. In many cases, especially in Judaism and Islam, there is a discomfort with traditions deemed as "idolatrous," based in the strictures found in the Bible and in the Qur'an. This challenge may be amplified if an event is held in a temple or other house of worship while images are present. Participation requires that, while this is neither one's own form of worship nor understanding of the divine, that other peoples and traditions worship and understand the divine in ways differing from our own. The aim of multi-faith events is not to change or challenge one's own beliefs about the divine or one's traditions or practices, but rather to educate and open one's mind to the diversity of human religious expression.

While joint prayer can serve to create an appreciation of the diversity of faith expressions, and often can be a bridge to building better relations between people from many traditions, it can also limit, implicitly, the ability to initiate some important multi-faith conversations. There are traditions that feel a strong discomfort with prayer events. Indeed, participation may be precluded by their beliefs and traditions, and the events themselves may be perceived as dangerous, or as having a hidden agenda. While they may choose, therefore, not to participate in joint prayer services, they may still be willing to participate in other educational events such as dialogues or presentations. While the unwillingness to participate in joint prayer may be seen by some as a rejection of the basic narratives for interfaith interaction, the openness to dialogue and hear of other traditions can be a necessary first step to coexistence and acceptance of difference.

IX

Moving from Tolerance to Appreciation

THE SEARCH FOR UNDERSTANDING AND COOPERATION WITHin our global society must begin with an acceptance of difference, in culture, religion, color, gender, and sexual orientation. Indeed, there are many venues across the world where this process takes place. Yet, often even in interfaith meetings that aim to bridge differences, the most complex issues are never examined. Right from the start mistakes are made that impede success, and assumptions, about language and use of symbols prevents us from seeing and understanding other peoples and traditions.

There is often an implicit assumption made that words and symbols have one meaning, easily understood by everyone within a society. While, to a great extent, there is truth to this assertion, for if not there wouldn't be any meaningful communication, there are many pitfalls to this assumption. The same word or symbol can carry a variety of connotations to people from different groups and ethnicities. The question, "when do you worship in your church," may seem innocent within a Christian context, for example, while it may be offensive to someone who worships in a synagogue, temple, mosque or gurdwara. Even less obviously religiously oriented words, such as grace or rapture, can also have very different meanings from one community to the next. It is therefore important to consider our language and our assumptions about meaning when we talk to people of other faiths.

Though many may not realize it the meaning of particular words and cultural symbols is not fixed. Instead, they are contextual, and complex. Semiotic theory (the study of the denotation of meaning) suggests that words, objects and symbols do not have fixed meaning. Yet, within a society, at a particular time and place, there is a relative consensus that allows for communication.

At its most basic level semiotics examines the relationship between signs and their meanings. Within a society, or group, people function through a variety of means of communication, be they sets of symbols or language, denoted by semiotics as mediums. When a medium is widely used within a culture group, it creates an almost unconscious layer of mediation between the person and the signs that he is using or interpreting, imposing to a great extent a meaning onto the sign. A medium can also shape the direction of thought or creation, because every medium has its own series of signs and methods, which limit the user of the medium, especially if he hopes to be understood by others.

The society or sub-group can also impose a degree of implicit mediation on the signs used within it. Words, even in the same language, can have very different meanings among communities in close proximity one to another. Rapture, for example, has a very different meaning when it is used by a pre-millennialist Christian than when it is used by a Jew living in the same general community. To the Christian it suggests that elevation of the elect to heaven prior to the tribulations of the apocalypse, while the Jew may well understand it as suggesting sexual bliss, or even merely extreme happiness. It is therefore important to look at the objects of communication (words, images, icons, etc.) not as having fixed meanings, but rather even within a single complex community rather as having large matrix of potential meanings.

Within a semiotic model signs are the constituent objects of thought. Human beings take objects, words, sounds and invest them with meaning. The sign is the combination of object and meaning, and these two constituent parts, denoted as the signifier and the signified are the basic units of semiotics. The signifier is the form of the sign, be it a word, gesture or an object. The signified is the concept that the sign represents. The relationship between these two is referred to as signification, whereby the signifier is invested by the one who sees or uses it with the signified, that is to say, meaning.

Meaning is created both by individual signs and also by combinations of signs. A sentence, for example, is a combination of signs, where the meaning of the whole is greater than the sum of its parts, because the signs that comprise the sentence affect each other and modify meaning. Within the context of language grammar provides a model that allows us to understand how these signs (words) function together to lend signification and understanding, thereby to create a meaningful whole. All groups of signs, from language to art have their own implicit grammar.

There is not, however, a one-to-one correspondence between signifier and signified, as the relationship between the two is totally arbitrary.

Meanings of signs within a single society are arbitrary in themselves, and also in their relationship with other signs. Indeed, there can be a multiplicity of meanings to a single sign. Within a single cultural group the meaning of a sign can change based on its proximity. The word [signifier] open, for example, if placed in the window of a store, signifies that the store is open for business, while if it is printed on the lid of a box, it can indicate how the box should be opened. Indeed, between cultural groups the meaning imposed on a signifier can be quite different. So, for example, for some people living in Canada white is a symbol of joy and purity, while for those of Japanese and Chinese descent, white is a sign of mourning, and perhaps in a third group present in our community it can mean nothing at all.

It is therefore dangerous to assume any meaning to a particular signifier, and to suggest that the meaning is fixed for all time since there is no intrinsic or necessary connection between the signifier and the signified. The word "sensibility" for example is a random combination of letters, we however invest it with arbitrary meanings through the process of signification, which is contextual and cultural, and both context and culture can change. To an Englishman living in the eighteenth century sensibility implied an excess of emotion, while to us it is the ability to appreciate and respond to complex emotional or aesthetic influences. As noted above in the examination of "rapture", it is clear that even within a larger community, sub-groups can invest a single signifier with a multiplicity of significations.

The crypto-Jews of the Southwest of the United States evidence an interesting example of the complexity of the construction in the meaning of symbols.[105] This community spans many world views, as a sub group within the larger Hispanic population, their identity is contested between American and Hispanic; through their crypto identity they are at once secretly Jewish and openly (for the most part) Catholic. Because of this complex identity the world view and therefore the interpretation of signs by the crypto-Jews is very different than that of the larger Hispanic

---

105 The crypto-Jews are a sub grouping of the Hispanic community. They are descendants of Jews forcible converted to Catholicism between 1390 and 1492, and are to be found in Spain, Portugal and throughout the Spanish diaspora. Many crypto-Jews retain a strong memory of their Jewish identity, and attempt to secretly practice a form of Judaism while ostensibly being Catholic Hispanics. This analysis is based on my paper "When is a Top Not Only a Top," given at the Conference of the Society for Crypto-Judaic Studies, 2007.

community, and that of both the Catholic and Jewish communities, yet they live within the same culture area with its shared language (Spanish),[106] history, and cultural objects. Through the process of *bricolage* the crypto-Jews invest cultural objects, such as a top or even a crucifix, with meanings that express their idiosyncratic world view, rather than that of the greater Hispanic population.

The *pon y seca*, a four-sided top, is a common cultural object found throughout the Hispanic community of the Southwest; for most it is merely a children's toy, but for the crypto-Jews it is a seen as a confirmation of their Jewish identity and it is identified with a dreidle (a toy used on Hanukkah by eastern European Jews). Historian Stan Hordes and Anthropologist Seth Kunin chart the process of ritual development and *bricolage* that transformed the *pon y seca* into a dreidle. Informants, claiming crypto-Judaic descent, described by Hordes and Kunin (Hordes, 2005: 248; Kunin, 2001: 56), clearly connect their usage of the *pon y seca* with Hanukkah and their Jewish identity, and suggest that its origins go back to the early years of the twentieth century – a time when Jews of Ashkenazic (Eastern European) origin could be found in New Mexico. They suggest, that it is not unlikely that crypto-Jews would consciously or unconsciously connect material from their own culture with a pre-existing customs from people easily identifiable as Jews (Kunin, 2001: 56). Kunin also suggests that connection of pon *y seca* as dreidle has now become an element of crypto-Judaic identity. It is now used during the winter months explicitly because of its perceived connection with the dreidle and therefore as a means of reinforcing and as an expression of Jewishness. He suggests that this is an example of conceptual *bricolage* (56).

Indeed, semiotics can add an additional layer to this analysis. Critics of the crypto-Judaic phenomena implicitly assume that the *pon y seca* has only one signified, universally accepted by all the people in the region. Yet, there is no reason to assume that this is necessarily true. The *pon y seca* is an arbitrary sign, to which a multiplicity of meanings can be attached, even within the same region or general community. Even if the *pon y seca* was once just a gambling top for all the Hispanic community that does not imply that the signification is fixed for all time. Indeed, as demonstrated above, signification can change over time, as communities

---

106 It has been suggested, however that some Crypto-Jewish families retained an older version of Spanish, not identical to that of the larger Hispanic community.

use and see the signs in new ways. The fact that crypto-Judaic informants now equate the signifier *pon y seca* with the signified "dreidle", and that it serves that purpose within their community lends it authenticity. To them (and for their ancestors who created the association), the *pon y seca* is indeed now a dreidle.

The process of *bricolage* and semiotic transformation, in relation to material culture among the crypto-Jews, is evident through other customs practiced by the crypto-Jews. Kunin identifies rituals, which exhibit a negotiation between concurrently living a Catholic and Jewish life (52-54). One of these includes an absolute transformation in the meaning of a sign. An informant reported that all the crypto-Jews in her village attempted to unobtrusively observe the Jewish tradition of affixing a *mezzuzah* on their doorposts. Instead, however, of using the traditional box and scroll (to which they would have no access, no specific knowledge, and could have posed significant danger), crucifixes were utilized. To them, the signifier crucifix no longer signified Christianity; instead it was subverted to signify their Jewish identity. This custom also exemplifies the process of *bricolage* as the community utilized baggage from their cultural milieu, and transformed it to fit with their underlying structure.

Another example of Crypto-Jewish negotiation between Catholic and Jewish identity can be seen in the creation and identification of *retablos* and *bulitos* (or *santos*)[107] as figures from the Hebrew Bible. These images are ubiquitous in communities that were part of the Spanish Empire, and are nearly always figures from the Christian Scriptures. In New Mexico, however, *retablos* and *bulitos* have both been created (and older figures have been reidentified) as saints with the unusual names of Job and Moses, both figures from the Hebrew Bible (Hordes 2002: 262-264).[108] The creation of these figural depictions may well be another example of *bricolage*, as the *santero* (the artist) consciously or unconsciously utilizes a form with is part of his cultural baggage, but transforms it to fit the structure of crypto-Jewish identity.

The complexities of language and symbols demonstrated here makes communication between differing traditions, world views and peoples difficult, because we need to move away from all preconceived notions,

---

107 *Retablos* are painted, and *bulitos* carved images, usually of saints.

108 The use of the title saint by sixteenth century crypto-Jews, from a number of locations in the Spanish Diaspora, in connection with figures from the Hebrew Bible is also mentioned also by David Gitlitz in his ground breaking work on the earliest Crypto-Jewish communities (Gitlitz, 2002: 117).

even to the meanings of the words we speak and symbols that we take for granted. After all, for the crypto Jew even the crucifix is a contested symbol. Symbols and rituals such as the lighting of candles can be positive in some traditions (as in, for example, Judaism, Christianity, Zoroastrianism and Wicca) while in others they can be viewed as negative (as in Islam). Even where the same ritual or symbol is present, it can also mean very different things. The swastika, for example, is a symbol of good luck for Buddhists, Hindus and Jains; for Nazis (and neo-Nazis) it was a symbol of their racist doctrine; for Jews it is a symbol of ultimate evil.

Language is also important in the implicit and explicit meanings that are attached to the words that we use. Words like tolerance, and even interfaith or interreligious send different messages. The search for tolerance is a catchword often used with reference to minorities, be they based on race, religion, gender or ethnicity. At first glance this seems an appropriate goal. Yet, words – and the meanings behind them – are important. Is tolerance truly the goal we seek when we come together to understand one another?

The primary definition of tolerance, as found in *Webster's New World Dictionary*, is, "Tolerating or being tolerant, especially of views, beliefs, practices, etc. of others that differ from one's own." The primary definition of "tolerating", that is "to not interfere with; allow, permit" helps to hone in on the true meaning of tolerance. Based on these definitions, tolerance could be defined as a majority culture of giving permission to others in their midst to practice their differing traditions and hold their diverse beliefs. In essence, then tolerance implies a policy of sufferance. The majority culture – realizing perhaps that those who are different culturally, racially, or religiously are present in their midst, and, without violent action, there to stay – generously decides to bear with their presence, and to allow them to maintain their differences. It does not imply, however, that the majority culture believes that these minority groups have any worth, or that there is any legitimacy to their beliefs or practices. Nor does it imply that their presence adds anything to the majority culture. A majority that merely tolerates minorities does not even indicate a desire to learn from or interact with members of those minorities.

The concept of tolerance is inextricably tied to concepts of ethnocentrism and cultural superiority. Indeed, imbedded within "tolerance," is a sense of power. The word suggests that "we" the majority have the right to decide who to allow or tolerate within our midst. Tolerance does not imply mutuality; rather it seems to carry with it an almost hostile co-existence without any necessary sense of permanence. For, though we may "allow" or "permit" you to exist with us today, allowances and permissions can be withdrawn sometime in the future. Tolerance, therefore, should have no place on the table when we come together to seek to understand one another. We should not merely be seeking ways to coexist as separate entities living on one land mass, where the more powerful permits the less powerful to survive. Rather, the goal should be mutual understanding and appreciation.

From the Jewish tradition this process could begin with an understanding that we are each part of the human race, created equally in the divine image (however we understand that). Other traditions will have diverse understandings of our mutuality and connections. It could be, for example that all humanity is part of and connected to the rest of the universe, implying not only an obligation of one human to another, but even more an obligation by all humanity for everything within the world. Whatever the basis of our understanding, however, if we are to survive we must work towards an appreciation of the multiplicity of differing paths that we take to express our humanity, and our common search for meaning and for the transcendent. Our language must express this goal, not as tolerating difference but as appreciating difference and diversity.

Many of the basic assumptions that we make are related to a concept of tolerance and moral superiority. As discussed earlier, the Golden Rule, for example, implies that the cultural morality of the majority is the right one for everyone. It implies that the majority definitions of ethics – of right and wrong behavior – are the correct definitions for all humanity. An example of such thinking was found on the pages of the *New York Times* Sunday magazine section's column called "The Ethicist." Each week the column deals with a variety of ethical questions. On October 27, 2002 the author of the column was asked the following question:

> *The courteous and competent real-estate agent I'd just hired to rent my house shocked and offended me when, after we signed our contracts, he refused to shake my hand, saying as an Orthodox Jew he could not touch women. As a feminist, I oppose sex discrimination of all sorts. However, I also support freedom of religious expression. How do I balance these conflicting values? (Cohen: 2002)*

The questioner clearly states the conflict of values. On one hand, she had her own strongly felt ideas about appropriate behavior, but on the other hand she valued the concept of a diversity of correct answers.

The author, Randy Cohen, answered this ethical dilemma through the implementation of the Golden Rule. He wrote that the questioner has the right to expect that her definition of respect for others (which Cohen connects with basic American values derived from the Constitution), takes precedence over the agent's religious values, and indeed the appropriate marks of respect found within another culture.

> *This culture clash may not allow you to reconcile the values you esteem. Though the agent dealt you only a petty slight, without ill intent, you're entitled to work with someone who will treat you with the dignity that he shows his male clients. [My emphasis.] … I believe you should tear up your contract.*

In essence, Cohen is telling her that rather than respecting cultural and religious differences, failure to follow American norms was sufficient to lead to the cancellation of the contract.[109]

Cohen clearly believes that American values constitute the epitome of human values, and therefore can be imposed on any who choose to live in the United States. People from other traditions and cultures are therefore tolerated rather than respected. A more respectful answer might have been phrased as follows:

> *This culture clash may not allow you to reconcile the values you esteem. Though the agent did not show respect as our culture defines it, he did not do this with any ill intent. Rather, he showed proper respect according to the traditional practices of his society, which differ from our own. Therefore, I believe that you should honor your contract.*

The concept and use of the term "appreciation of difference" asks us to broaden our minds, and to move beyond the idea that our culture has all the answers for appropriate human behavior. The use of this language allows us to escape from the "us" verse "them" power dichotomy, placing every tradition on an equal footing.

---

109 It could be argued that the realtor also refused to respect the norms of the other. However, the questioner makes it clear that he showed her all possible respect within the parameters permitted him within his religious tradition. It is interesting to note that responses to this Ethicist Column from across the Jewish spectrum called Cohen to task for his answer.

The assumption of cultural superiority and mere tolerance can lead to a failure to respect basic differences at the outset, which leads most likely to a failure of the entire interaction. Food rules and rules of contact between the sexes are merely two examples of areas where cultural norms can come into conflict. At the outset of discussion we may not even be aware of all the differences, but we must be open to learning about them, and then to respecting them.

A level of sophistication is necessary as we live and work in a global society with peoples from many other traditions and cultures. Stereotypes, even ones that may be considered as positive (Jews argue/heatedly discuss everything, Asians are industrious, etc.), are both largely untrue and prevent us from seeing the uniqueness of the other as we lose ourselves in our own preconceived notions. Often we are trapped by our own underlying baggage of thought and become captive of stereotypes learned through our upbringing, environment and education. The challenge one faces is to get beyond one's stereotypes, and to see the other as he or she is, rather than we how we want them or expect them to be.

Yet, even meals create challenges built on assumptions of cultural uniformity, as well as opportunities for constructive conversation. Since there are few food taboos within the dominant Christian-American milieu, the assumption is often made that the same is true of other religions. Even at times where food rules are recognized, observers are placed in a second-class status, eating only a special vegetarian appetizer, while everyone else eats a forbidden main course. There may also be discomfort of eating at a table where forbidden food is also being consumed. In any of these cases, the comfort necessary for communication is precluded.

It is for this reason, namely, the creation of opportunities for true interaction, which is essential that we take into account not only the factors examined above but also the implicit and explicit messages that we send by means of the environment that we chose to create. Food can simultaneously bring people together and also can push people away. Indeed, culturally food laws serve exactly this purpose. *Kashrut* (the Jewish food rules), for example, not only helps to create a sense of cohesiveness and community between observant Jews, it also tends to raise barriers for similar relationships with the outside world. Our goal should be to achieve the first of these objectives, to bring diverse people together providing them with the comfort and confidence necessary both for dialogue and the development of true relationships.

While food rules of the major religious traditions vary, they can be divided into two major categories, restrictions on the consumption of animal products and the consumption of stimulants and/or alcoholic beverages.

Dietary Restrictions of World Religions[110]

- Buddhism: Many Buddhists are vegetarian.
- Hinduism: Beef is prohibited and vegetarianism is a preferred option. Many Hindus avoid alcoholic beverages.
- Islam: Pork, certain birds and Alcohol are prohibited. Meat must be slaughtered according to the rules of Halal.[111]
- Judaism: Pork, Shellfish and certain birds are prohibited. Milk and meat may not be consumed together. Food products must have Kashrut certification.[112]
- Mormonism: Alcoholic beverages, and beverages containing caffeine are prohibited.
- Protestants: Some denominations forbid the use of alcoholic beverages.
- Adventists: Seventh Day Adventists prohibit pork products, vegetarianism is encouraged and coffee, tea and alcoholic beverages are forbidden.

This list represents only a small fraction of religions with traditions concerning the consumption of food. But even this small sample represents the complexity of creating an environment conducive to building bridges of understanding. As we wrestle with the appropriate responses to the various traditions surrounding food it is essential that we understand these prohibitions from the perspective of the individual religions for which they are important, rather than from an academic

---

[110] Please note, this chart is not comprehensive. For greater detail resources from the religious traditions should be consulted. Within any religious tradition there will be variations on the level of observance of these food restrictions.

[111] In order for food to be considered halal, it must not be a forbidden substance and any meat, must have been slaughtered according to traditional guidelines set forth by the Sunnah, known as *dhabiha*. Some Islamic authorities allow the consumption of kosher meat others do not.

[112] In order for food to be certified kosher, it must not be a forbidden substances, must not contain and mixture of milk and meat products, and any meat must have been slaughtered according to traditional guidelines and under rabbinic supervision. Kosher food must be prepared in a kitchen that is properly cleaned and supplied to maintain the separation between milk and meat. In areas where kosher food is not easily available many Jews will be willing to eat a vegetarian meal.

or other external framework. While some groups may base their food traditions on understandings of health, others may root their rituals in commands from the Divine. It is also dangerous to look at individual practice to draw conclusions for an entire community. Even if some or many adherents are not strict in their observance of these dietary rules, it does not follow that they therefore are of no importance and need not be respected.

The Sikh *langur* (communal meal/soup kitchen) provides one of the best examples of a meal designed so for the comfort of everyone. The *Langur*, a tradition instituted by Guru Nanak (the first Sikh Guru) is found at every Sikh *Granthi* (temple) and is open to people of all faiths. From its institution in the fifteenth century the food provided has been completely vegetarian, thus allowing anyone to feel comfortable while eating. Sikhism, despite having no formal food restrictions of its own, was founded in a milieu of largely Muslims, Hindus, Jains and Buddhist peoples each with their own complex food traditions. Guru Nanak created the *langur* as a place where people from all of these traditions could come, eat together and dialogue without having either to break with their tradition or to feel discomfort in the presence of that which was forbidden.

X

Challenging My Own Tradition

WITHIN NEARLY EVERY TRADITION, AND JUDAISM IS NO exception; there are significant challenges to successful and open participation in interfaith interaction. For some, long histories of persecution and victimization make trust difficult, while for others the modern political reality, for example the Arab - Israeli conflict (which after 9/11 has unfortunately become perceived as a West verses Muslim conflict) also creates difficulties in acceptance and communication. Traditional texts and doctrines stressing absolute truth, which denies the possibility of the truth of any other faith, also can prevent open interaction. Those who are interested and committed to interfaith interaction therefore need to honestly confront and transcend the impediments within their own traditions.

The Jewish approach to interfaith is challenged by each of these impediments. After nearly two thousand years of persecution, marked by a series of horrific events culminating in the Holocaust, many Jews are unready to trust people of other faiths – especially Christians and ironically Muslims (see below), and all interfaith overtures are seen with skeptical eyes. Motivations are questioned and overtures may be seen as hidden forms of proselytization. Jews, as a very small minority (with the exception of Israel) within pervasive majority cultures largely perceived as Christian fear that interfaith interaction will hasten assimilation and the subsequent loss of identity. This fear is especially pervasive in the United States and Canada, countries where ironically Jews feel and are the most comfortable and accepted.

The modern geo-political situation has also complicated Jewish relations with other religious traditions. The Arab - Israeli conflict, has created an "us versus them" dichotomy, complicating Jewish and Muslim relations. It is ironic that this conflict is now granted iconic status, because the condition of the Jewish minority in the Islamic world was far better, for most of the last one and a half millennia (Muhammad died in 632 C.E.), than in Christian nations. Indeed, in extreme periods of persecution (the Spanish pogroms of the 1390's and the Spanish expulsion in 1492) Jews fled from Christian countries to areas largely under the control of the Muslim Ottoman Empire. The Arab - Israeli conflict also complicates Jewish-Christian relations as Jews express both distrust and disappointment of various Christian denominational condemnations of Israel.[113]

Despite these impediments, there is significant dialogue and interaction between Jews, Christians and Muslims. The age-old persecutions and modern conflicts, as well as the proximity of the three traditions have provided an impetus, and indeed a sense of necessity, to the interaction. The relative ease of the interaction is also strengthened by the "Abrahamic Faiths" narrative, which stresses the historic and ideological relationship of the three traditions. Each is perceived as worshiping the same vision of the divine (the God of Abraham), and in sharing some familial connection with the patriarch Abraham.[114] This narrative creates a broad dichotomy of religions, namely, the three Abrahamic traditions verses all the rest. The other traditions are viewed as potentially pagan or idolatrous, and as worshiping something other than God.[115]

---

113 The recent (2012) decision by the United Church of Canada to boycott products originating from Israeli settlements on the West Bank, and the subsequent strong reaction by the Canadian Jewish community exemplify this point. See, for example, www.gc41.ca/sites/default/files/reports_79-124.pdf (the United Church position paper) and http://www.cija.ca/issues/ucc/ (the Jewish reaction).

114 While there is general consensus within the Jewish legal literature that Islam is a monotheistic and non-idolatrous religion there is less consensus concerning Christianity. Maimonides suggests that it is idolatrous (commentary on *Mishnah Avodah Zarah* 1:4), an opinion echoed as recently as the twentieth century by the prominent Orthodox authority, R. Moshe Feinstein (*Igrot Moshe, Yoreh De'ah, v. 3, n. 129)*. Other legal sources, on the other hand, view Christianity as monotheistic (see both the tosefot on *Avodah Zarah* 2a, and the thirteenth century Hameiri (also on *Avodah Zarah*). This view is likewise supported in the twentieth century by Isaac Halevi Herzog (*Shana Beshana*, 1986, pp. 136-140, and by Conservative authority Elliot Dorff (2005: 523-526)

115 The focus on Jewish, Christian and Muslim relations is also attributable to the perceived challenges facing the Jewish community. The fact that outside of Israel most Jews live in Christian countries gives impetus to create better relations between faiths, especially after nearly 2000 years of persecution, and the persistence of anti-Semitism. The Arab - Israeli conflict also gives relevance

The potential negative categorization of traditions outside the Abrahamic fold is biblical in origin – these texts and/or ideas are shared by all three traditions. The biblical authors perceived the world as a conflict between a monotheistic Israelite nation and the idolatrous nations that surrounded her. It was seen as a life and death struggle, where survival depended on the destruction of all pagan symbols within the Israelite polity. Over the millennia, though contexts changed, these laws have become a historical relic of the past that has left its mark on the Jewish tradition. Even today they form the context of relations between the Jewish tradition and other religions, especially for traditional (mainly Orthodox) Judaism. While many have come to see Islam and Christianity as monotheistic religions, and therefore, relatively acceptable, it has been more difficult to accept or engage in dialogue with other traditions which are perceived as worshiping images or a multiplicity of gods.

The author has identified one Orthodox source – one of the few from any of the major movements of Judaism – that examines an engagement with Hinduism, perceived by many as a polytheistic religion. Rabbi Daniel Sperber, describes the encounter as focusing on the question as to whether Hinduism was indeed polytheistic (Sperber, 2009).[116] During the course of discussion, the Hindu religious leaders denied this assumption, claiming that there was only an outward manifestation of polytheism and idolatry. There was, they explained, one divine power that expressed itself in many ways – expressed through the idea of a multiplicity of gods. This explanation allowed Sperber, the other rabbinic delegates and the Hindu leaders to view the event as a success, and to issue a joint statement. While this document reflects a courageous stand within the context of Jewish orthodoxy, it also reflects the need to see "ourselves" – in this case the embrace of a single god – in others as a necessary element of acceptance. It is clear that the summit was viewed as successful, from Sperber's point of view, only because the Hinduism was also expressed as ultimately a monotheistic tradition. [117]

---

to Jewish - Muslim dialogue.

116 Sperber is president of Machon haGavoah leTorah at Bar Ilan University. Bar Ilan is an Orthodox University (perceived within the Orthodox world as modern or moderate) in Israel.

117 Within the Orthodox world acceptance of Hinduism, even with the understanding that it is ultimately monotheistic, is not universal. See, for example, the response to Sperber by Rabbi Shabtai ha-Cohen Rappaport (Sperber: 2009). Rabbi Rappaport suggests, based on Maimonides, that Hinduism is still

These laws and traditions speak both of a fear and distrust of the other and of a belief that the Jewish tradition has the only correct and unique understanding of the divine – shared perhaps to a lesser extent by the Abrahamic club. These prohibitions developed to prevent the assimilation of pagan ideas, practices and beliefs within the Israelite polity. They reflect the fear that any minority may feel in regards to a pervasive majority. They also reflect a lack of self-confidence both in the Jewish belief system, and in Jews choosing to remain true to their tradition. This fear and distrust was amplified by the anti-Semitism and persecution fueled by xenophobia especially in Christian Europe. Yet, the goal of modern interfaith dialogue (as opposed to debate)[118] and interaction is not conversion, but rather understanding and acceptance. Ignorance and stereotype in our global community are far more dangerous than knowledge of the "other."

Within the more traditional wings of Judaism and even within official statements of the middle-of-the-road Conservative movement, this distrust of the other and fear of those deemed idolatrous shapes official discourse on interfaith relations. There is, for example, no official utterance, that the author could find, from any of the major movements concerning interfaith relations beyond the "Abrahamic Faiths."[119] When discussed, these traditions (and even at times the other "Abrahamic Faiths) are often placed within the Jewish narrative of the seven

---

"idolatry" though perhaps also monotheistic.

118 Modern Interfaith dialogue should not be confused with the medieval and early modern confrontations, labeled as dialogue, which were largely an exercise of power and coercion, as discussed below, p. 98.

119 There is no doubt that rabbis from the Reform, Conservative and Reconstructionist movements participate in dialogue, which extends beyond the "Abrahamic Faiths." Even, as noted above, some Orthodox rabbis do so as well. Official statements, however, especially in the area of *halakhah* (Jewish Law) appear to be uniformly silent on this issue. A recent work of Conservative *responsa* (Susskind Goldberg and Villa, 2010: 83-96) includes a section entitled "Interfaith Issues, which focuses entirely on the "Abrahamic" traditions, see most notably, p. 93. After categorically stating that Muslims and Christians are not considered idolaters, they make the surprising claim that "it is rare to find people who actually worship idols." This statement goes without any explanation, and still leaves a potential for the category of "idolatry." The most widely quoted Orthodox response, issues by Rabbi J. B. Soloveitchik entitled "Confrontation," likewise deals only with the "Abrahamic" traditions – in this case only Christianity.

Noachide laws. These are the laws traditional Jews believe were given to Noah and his children (some suggest that most of these laws were given to Adam), and therefore all the nations of the world (Sanhedrin 56a).[120] The Noachide laws include prohibitions against idolatry, murder, theft, sexual immorality, blasphemy, and the eating of meat taken from a live animal. The seventh law calls for the establishment of courts of justice. The Jewish tradition claims that those who follow these laws, even if they are from a idolatrous religion, fall into the category of the righteous of the world; a grouping, which is guaranteed a place in the world to come (Sanhedrin 105a).

While many of these may seem logical and can be seen as an example of God's commitment to the entirety of creation, to my mind the entire Noachide system stems from the ethnocentric concept of a unitary truth, which is in the sole possession of the Jewish people. The Noachide tradition forces the rest of humanity into an imposed structure and series of definitions. People are categorized and understood based on a very limited set of criteria, and are seen only through the lens of Judaism, rather than as they would like to be seen or understood. Indeed, both the Golden Rule and the Noachide laws are examples of narratives of essential message, where a single tradition imposes that which it sees as essential on every other world religion. Such a narrative, can comfort those who feel confirmation of their tradition through its imposition, but it provides no help in understanding and accepting other traditions on their own terms.

The fear of other traditions is also found in the Jewish response to events featuring prayer from many faiths. Recently the Orthodox community condemned Haskel Lookstein, a prominent Orthodox rabbi, for participating in an Interfaith prayer service celebrating the election of Barak Obama – the condemnation was based both on his participation (which gave tacit acceptance of the legitimacy of "idolatrous" religions), but also on his presence in the National Cathedral (many Orthodox and even Conservative authorities forbid Jews from entering churches) (Grossman, 2009). Similarly, Conservative rabbis, Goldberg and Villa, while accepting the legitimacy of such prayer events, believing that they allow for shared spiritual experience, impose a series of conditions that need to pertain for Jewish participation.[121] The prayers included in the

---
120 See also, Tosefta Avodah Zarah 8:4 and Genesis Rabbah 34:8.
121 This last condition is based on the lack of consensus within Jewish sources, both ancient and modern, on the permissibility of a Jew entering and

service, they suggest, must be neutral and agreed upon by and the participants. The service should also be held in a neutral space. While these conditions are more accepting of other religions than the Orthodox response, they leave little room for authenticity – or it could be argued spirituality. They also prevent participants to gain a greater understanding of other traditions (Goldberg and Villa, pp. 93-94).[122]

These challenges to full engagement by Jews in interfaith interaction are based, at least to some extent, by our liturgy, surprisingly in both the traditional and liberal wings of the Jewish tradition. Prayers, examined in detail later in this chapter, bolster the old certainties and beliefs in absolute truths, which can blind us to the potential for the authenticity of other religions. As Jews we often look to other world traditions demanding inclusiveness and pluralism, yet within our own tradition we constantly speak and pray with the language not only of being "chosen" but superiority. Can we truly look to our tradition as a means of creating a world of peace when through our daily prayers we send explicit and implicit messages that deny the legitimacy of all others?[123]

Liturgy can often be one of the most conservative aspects of religious life, changing much more slowly than other areas of practice or belief, remaining, on occasion, out of touch with changing values. Thus, there are many areas (especially in the traditional *siddur* – prayer book) where our liturgy is not consonant with modern understandings of tolerance, respect and appreciation of religious diversity. Yet, these prayers are read on a daily and weekly basis.[124] We have reacted strongly to the inclusion

---

church or mosque. Sources are unambiguous that it is forbidden to enter temples of traditions beyond the Abrahamic faiths.

122 For a more detailed examination of interfaith prayer see Chapter 7, "Narratives of Prayer."

123 The concept of "chosen people" is not addressed below. While it can be seen as an expression of both elitism and triumphalism, it can also be understood as a belief that God chose the Jewish people for a particular task. This understanding does not preclude the possibility that God can also choose other peoples for different tasks.

124 Many of these same arguments can be adduced when examining the traditional cycle of weekly Torah and Haftarah (drawn from the prophetic books of the bible) readings. The consecutive reading of the entire Torah was clearly fixed from antiquity (whether triennial or annual) and the mandated weekly reading, even with unpalatable messages, must be used. These might include texts that command us to destroy enemies, or break down their altars. These messages, should however be ameliorated from the pulpit. The Haftarah cycle, while also ancient, may present a greater opportunity for change. The precedent

of belittling words used against us in the liturgy other traditions.[125] Yet, we are silent as similar words are used in our own.

It could be argued that it is unnecessary for prayer always to reflect changing values, as it has different purposes. Liturgy serves to connect us with our past as we pray with the words of generations of our ancestors. Prayer can also challenge the very ideas it presents, as it provides the opportunity for us to ruminate on ideas that have been set forth as normative, demanding that we confront them and consider how they work in our own lives and world view. It could also be argued that the very pluralism espoused here requires that we maintain a variety of perspectives within our liturgy, rather than eject disfavored ideas.

While these arguments are attractive, they fail to take into account one of the most significant features of prayer. Prayer may connect us to the past, yet few would claim that prayer primarily functions as a memorial to our ancestors. The words of our prayers are not an empty connector to the past. Rather we believe that they have intrinsic merit, which, hopefully, affects the way we respond to God and the world.[126] It is also unlikely that the inclusion of "triumphalist" prayers will lead an adherent to challenge his or her inherent world view. People are challenged not by texts that tend to create a sense of comfort (in this case that the adherent and his or her tradition is better than all others), rather they are challenged when a text confronts their complacency and attacks their sense of comfort. The argument that prayers expressing "triumphalist" theologies should remain as an expression of diversity of opinion is likewise flawed. Acceptance of diversity demands respect for the other, and cannot be used to justify texts that undermine that basic respect. Therefore, the transformative power of prayer, with implicit and explicit messages, militates against the continuity of usage of prayers, which express mes-

---

of occasional differing readings in Ashkenazic and Sephardic rites may be sufficient to allow for the choice of new alternative readings. A precedent was also set both in the Harlow and *Lev Shalom* High Holiday prayer books with the introduction of alternative Torah and Haftarah readings.

125 See, for example, the recent response (2007) by the Anti Defamation League to a decree by Pope Benedict allowing the use of the old form of the Mass, which calls upon God to "lift the veil of ignorance from the Jews. Abraham Foxman called this decision a body blow to Jewish-Catholic relations (http://web.israelinsider.com/Articles/Diplomacy/11640.htm).

126 A postmodern understanding of the written word (in this case Jewish liturgy) suggests that the only meaning that can be ascribed to a text is that discovered by the reader.

sages that can be seen as rising to a level of offensiveness both to our own ideals and to other peoples and traditions.

Within the Jewish tradition, prayer is seen as transformative and self-reflexive, challenging us as individuals and as communities to be the best that we can be. When we pray, we thank God for the world both as it is and as it could be. Within the traditional life prayer is the most regular of *halakhic* practices as each Jew is commanded not only to pray the three required services (*shacharit*, *mincha* and *maariv*) but also on many others occasions throughout the day (e.g. before and after eating). As such, the words of our liturgy form a constant refrain throughout our lives.[127]

Traditionally the rote repetition of both prayer and the other *mitzvot* has been defended with the rationalization that repetitive observance can one day lead to meaningful and intentional observance. This theory is based on the realization that as we consistently perform a ritual or read a prayer we increase the chance that the observance will become internalized and meaningful. It is a recognition that the things that we do and or pray/read over and over again, especially those which are invested with an aura of holiness, speak to and influence our unconscious thoughts. They shape us, even though we don't realize that we are being shaped. The words that we pray have the power to unconsciously reinforce both positive and negative concepts found within our tradition and lives. [128]

There are many ways of looking at our prayers, while some focus on their words; others loose themselves a mystical ecstasy where meaning has no importance. Yet, Heschel reminds us that the words of our prayers are important. He states, "That the words of our prayers are commitments, we stand for what we utter" (Heschel, 1983: 30). Indeed he bemoans the fact that for many today, the words of prayer no longer impel our actions (30).

We begin the *Amidah* with a meditation including the words, "may the words of my mouth and the meditation of my heart be acceptable to You my Rock and my Redeemer. The author of this text realized that

---

127 Prayer may also be the most regular *mitzvah* (commandment) observed by most modern Jews who chose not to live in a traditional life style. In many cases attendance at a synagogue service, and therefore the recitation of the traditional liturgy, is the primary form of observance.

128 It is for this reason that words like gypped, jewing down and Indian giver are pernicious. Such words implicitly reinforce negative stereotypes, which can undermine a society built on mutual respect. The move towards gender-neutral language in Reform, Conservative and Reconstructionist liturgy (especially in English translations) is a recognition of the power of language.

we pray on many levels, both explicit and implicit. All are important, because they both shape the reality of who we are and what we believe.

Indeed, prominent anthropologist Clifford Geertz argues that one of religion's primary roles is the conscious and unconscious shaping of the values and world view of the adherent. Geertz states that religion is one of the primary cultural systems for the maintenance and communication of societal structures. He defined religion as, "a system of symbols [in our case prayers] which acts to establish powerful, pervasive and long-lasting moods and motivations in men by formulating conceptions of a general order of existence and clothing these conceptions with such an aura of factuality that the moods and motivations seem uniquely realistic" (Kunin, 2003: 153). Religion through its symbols and rites gives a societal value, such as the particularistic and triumphalistic world view addressed here, the aura of "divine" truth. As such, the value becomes accepted without question.

The traditional daily repetition of the blessing *shelo asani isha* (who has not made me a woman), for example, especially as it is connected with similarly negatively phrased blessings concerning the other nations and slavery, serves to reinforce and give divine sanction to ideas about the second class status of woman within Orthodox Jewish life.[129] Orthodox Judaism – and indeed all forms of pre-nineteenth century Judaism – perceive women as ontologically inferior to men in the eyes of God and the tradition in a similar way that slaves are perceived as inferior to free people.[130] The daily repetition of the blessing explicitly reinforces wom-

---

129 The three blessings have their origin in the Talmud, *Men. 43b*, which currently reads, "R. Meir used to say: A man is obligated to recite these three blessings every day, they are as follows: 'who has made me a Jew,' 'who has not made me a woman,' and 'who has not made me a boor.' ... R. Acha bar Yaakov ... [said] 'who has not made me a slave.'" It has been suggested that the positive formulation 'who has made me a Jew' was an emendation to the printed *Vilna Shas* (the authoritative traditional printed edition of the Babylonian Talmud) changing the suggested original negative version of the prayer (as found in traditional prayer books) which might appear as offensive to non-Jews. Versions in the Tosephta (an ancient collection of rabbinic texts) and the Jerusalem Talmud include the more recognized text, 'who has not made ne a gentile' (see, for example, *T. Berachot* 6.23). The text in the Vilna Talmud seemingly adds stress to the two negative blessings there their juxtaposition with the positively formulated blessing.

130 Shaya Cohen adduces a number of texts, which epitomize the traditional view of the ontological inferiority of women, suggesting that it is due to their inability to be circumcised as they lack a phallus (Cohen, 2005: 135-141).

en's effective exclusion both from organized ritual life and from acting as full individuals within the eyes of the law – e.g., women may not serve as witnesses, act as judges or initiate a divorce.[131]

The implicit message of this blessing as well as the other negatively phrased blessings included in *Birkhot Ha-Shahar* was ameliorated by Silverman (and also in later Conservative prayer books) with a significant emendation. Each blessing was rephrased with the positive wording "who has made me..." In the most current Conservative prayer books the blessing concerning gender now reads, *she-asani b'zalmo* (who has made me in the divine image) (Feld, 2010: 37; Reisner, 2009: 6). The rephrased blessing now teaches the implicit message of gender equality as male and female are equally created in the image of God.[132]

Male slaves, on the other hand can be circumcised. While it could be argued that slaves were not considered as ontologically inferior to free people, as they could be receive their manumission, in many societies, both ancient and modern (including both ancient Rome and nineteenth century America) the freed man rarely had the same rights as one born free.

131 Some modern feminist Orthodox women (and Orthodox male apologists) argue that men and women are equal in traditional Judaism, but that they exist in separate spheres. The male's sphere is public, and they are therefore obligated to the time bound commandments, while the women's sphere is largely private, focused on the family. They are therefore differently obligated. Within this interpretive mode, these blessings are not seen as pejorative; rather, they are understood as expressing gratitude for distinctions in levels of obligation. The three blessings create a structure of non-Jews, slaves, Jewish women, and Jewish men each having their own obligations to God. The Jewish man, therefore, thanks God that he is not a woman because women are not obligated for the time-bound commandments, while Jewish men are so obligated (*Men. 43b*, Schottenstien Edition, 2003: note 43.)

Interestingly, the author of this note seems not to find this traditional understanding convincing as he also adds a long aside, pointing out the ways that women are spiritually superior to men. This modern positive interpolation is weakened, however, by the text of the Talmud. When asked why a blessing concerning women and slaves are both necessary – as their obligations vis-à-vis the mitzvoth is identical – R. Acha responds "that a slave is more debased than a woman" (*Men. 44a*). It can be inferred from this answer that in at least R. Acha's mind a Israelite woman is likewise 'more debased' than a Jewish man.

132 The implication of Genesis 1:27 that both genders were created in the image of God cannot be taken for granted within traditional Jewish texts. Cohen adduces several examples from medieval and ancient sources where women are seen as not being created in the divine image (Cohen: 50).

In a similar way, the modern inclusion, in *Siddur Sim Shalom* (Reisner: 36b) and other non-Orthodox prayer books, of the matriarchs in the first blessing of the *Amidah* has an implicit message, reinforced at each repetition of the prayer. The inclusion of women in this important prayer can be a reminder of the importance of all our ancestors no matter their gender, it can reinforce the legitimacy of gender equal leadership in the modern community, and it can serve as an encouragement for all Jews, no matter their sex, to play a full role in the religious life of their synagogue. Through the emendation of these words the Conservative liturgy now communicates and reinforces a new understanding of the role of women in society. It also recognizes and legitimates the changed status of women in modern society, establishing it as the status quo.

Prayers concerning the relative status of the Jewish people and the nations or Judaism vis-a-vis other world religions raise equally troubling questions as the gender related texts, yet Conservative liturgy has not responded to these questions. How would, for example, the Jewish community react if another major religion retained a curse, which could be interpreted as relating to us, as part of a major liturgical section of their prayer book? Unlike Reform and Reconstructionist *siddurim*, where many of these prayers have (at least in the past) been removed or significantly reworded[133], our liturgy retains unedited versions of such texts.[134] We have been diffident about editing or removing significant prayers from the *siddur*, citing issues of *halakha* (law) and *klal yisrael* (community). Ultimately, however, arguments of tradition, *halakhic* authority and even community cohesion are insufficient in the defense of either bigotry or the retention of prayers, which can lead to or justify the hatred of oth-

---

133 Three prayers, as examined below, have moved in and out of Reform and Reconstructionist *siddurim* (prayer books). While the *Birkat Haminim* (12th prayer of the traditional Amidah) was not included in either the Reform *Union Prayer Book* (1940), *Gates of Prayer* (1975) or the Reconstructionist *Daily Prayer* (1948), a version has been included both in the new Reform *Mishkan T'filah* (2008) and Reconstructionist *Kol Haneshamah* (2006). The second prayer examined below, "You have not given...", is not included in any Reform or Reconstructionist prayer book; while the third, the traditional wording of the *Aleinu* prayer (as edited in the seventeenth century) was excluded from the *Union Prayer Book* and *Daily Prayer*, but has likewise found its way back as an option in the later Reform and Reconstructionist *siddurim*.

134 In some cases translations are included which minimize the animus of the prayers, examined below, but the original Hebrew text is retained, implying somehow that if we don't understand what we are reading it can't be hurtful.

ers. These are certainly not messages that we would chose to reinforce as acceptable "divinely" sanctioned societal norm.

While other prayers could also be included, three major prayers are examined below, a blessing from the Weekday *Amidah*, a thematic passage from the Shabbat *Amidah* (not a blessing) and a liturgical segment (likewise not a blessing) not included in the *Amidah*. These prayers are emblematic of differing types of prayers in the traditional liturgy, and the analysis found below should be seen in a broader context, examining the possibility of emendation of other prayers found in our liturgy.[135]

Perhaps the most egregiously offensive prayer is included as the twelfth prayer in the weekday *Amidah*. The prayer, entitled *Birkat Haminim* (Blessing for the Heretics) calls on God to quickly destroy all His enemies, and concludes with the phrase, "Blessed are You, God, who smashes his enemies and humbles the insolent."[136] In this prayer we look to God as an instrument of vengeance against our enemies, however, the enemies upon which it focuses its horrors are not persecutors but rather those who disagree with us religiously.

While the traditional origin of the *Amidah* or *Sh'moneh Esreh* (Eighteen Benedictions) is shrouded in mystery, some texts attribute it to the later prophets (*Sifre to Deuteronomy 343*), to the elders of the great assembly (*Meg. 17b*) and to Rabban Gamaliel II (*Meg. 18b*) the tradition regarding author and origin of the *Birkat Haminim* (the twelfth blessing of the *Amidah*) is less ambiguous. The Talmud states (*Ber. 29b*) that Samuel the Younger at the request of Rabban Gamaliel composed this blessing. While there is scholarly debate about the actual makeup of the original *Amidah*, Elbogen and others, for example, suggest that originally there were only seventeen blessings and the addition of *Birkat Haminim* led to the name *Sh'moneh Esreh* (Elbogen, 1993: 33-37)[137] within the Talmudic tradition itself the *Birkat Haminim* was seen as an additional prayer (a nineteenth benedic-

---

135 Detailed Jewish legal argumentation is not included here. For thise interested in a more complete *halakhic* discussion see my article published in *Conservative Judaism*, "Rethinking Jewish Liturgy," (Kunin, 2013).

136 The English translation of the blessing included in *Siddur Sim Shalom* (Reisner: 39) tones down the language of the prayer, describing God as merely one who "humbles the arrogant." The Hebrew text, however, retains the traditional language of "smashing enemies."

137 Elbogen suggests that the fourteenth benediction (a blessing for Jerusalem and the messiah) was divided into two blessings at a later period.

tion), composed to deal with a historical reality, added to a preexisting eighteen blessing *Amidah*.[138]

In the context of the *sugya* (Talmudic discussion) it is unclear at whom the curse is aimed, as the original language of the blessing is not included nor does the existing printed text unambiguously identify the heretics.[139] Within scholarly literature it has been variously assigned to Judeo-Christians, Gnostics and other Jewish sectarians (Boyarin, 2006: 67-72). Indeed, the lack of specificity of the current version of the blessing has allowed some contemporary Orthodox thinkers to identify the heretics in more modern terms, as the "pernicious elements within our people...who have become estranged from true Judaism," which can be taken as referring, perhaps, to the Reform, Conservative and Reconstructionist movements (Hoffman, 1998: 135).

It is clear that the addition of this prayer to the preexisting *Amidah* (whether seventeen or eighteen blessings) was necessitated by a perceived threat from heretical groups whose members where part of existing Jewish congregations. The inclusion of this prayer in the *Amidah* would tend to exclude them, and create a sense of "inside" and "outside" both by its explicit wording and by the inability – or unwillingness – of a "heretic" to recite the words of the blessing.[140] Indeed, Maimonides explicitly states that the blessing was added because, "In the days of Rabban Gamaliel the heretics increased in Israel. They distressed Israel and incited them to abandon God. When [Rabban Gamaliel] saw this... his court arose and established a blessing which would contain a request of God to destroy the heretics" (Maimonides, MT *Hilkhot. T'fillah* 2:1). In his view, the rabbis of Yavnah added the prayer as a means

---

138 The *sugya* (Talmudic discourse) on *Ber. 28b* includes a late Babylonian question and response posed in the name of Rabbi Levi, which states explicitly that the *Birkat Haminim* was added as an additional blessing to the preexisting eighteen in Yavneh.

139 The printed Vilna edition of the Talmud calls it a blessing against the Sadducees, which is thought to be a late emendation made in response to pressure from the church (Dikdukei Soferim). Elbogen lists the following as variants in a variety of rites: apostates, sectarians and Christians (Elbogen: 45-46).

140 The hope that an unwillingness to recite the blessing would serve as a deterrent and as a mode of exclusion is illustrated ironically in the *sugya*. Following the blessing's completion its author, Samuel the Younger, forgets its wording. The text asks if he should be removed from acting as a leader of prayer since due to his forgetfulness it can be concluded that he, himself, has become a heretic (*Ber. 29a*).

of preserving the community in the light of contemporary internal and external threats.

The placement of a prayer asking that God curse our religious enemies, whoever they may be, within the most important section of the weekday services is antithetical to all that we as modern Jews value within our modern pluralistic society, where we embrace the concept that there are a multiplicity of authentic paths to the divine. While praying the *Amidah* one is considered to be in the very presence of God, and one is commanded to concentrate on each of its words. A pious member of the community is likely to hear and/or recite this prayer up to five times each day. It is unlikely or impossible that its repeated sentiments, placed into such a context, will have no effect on the attitude of those who take Jewish prayer seriously.

It is not unwarranted to suggest that as both the realities and attitudes (both towards other faiths and to dissenters within our own tradition) have changed, a blessing thus added could also be removed from the Amidah. Indeed, even in its most narrow reading, the inclusion of this blessing in Jewish prayer encourages internal bigotry vilifying the very diversity of religious expression, which is such an important part of the modern Jewish community.

A second liturgical segment, from the Shabbat Morning *Amidah*, can similarly be seen as offensive to modern sensibilities and to the value of respect for other religious traditions, though in this case the prayer doesn't call on God for violence. The text begins with the words, "You have not granted this day, *Adonai* our God, to the other peoples of the world, nor have you granted it, our Sovereign, as a heritage to idolaters. Nor do others share in its rest." (Harlow, 1983: 117.) It could be argued that this prayer is a celebration of a Jew's unique relationship with God while not denying the validity of other relationships. It is contended here, however, that the threefold repetition of denial, "You have not granted…nor have you granted it…nor do others share" raises this prayer both to the level of triumphalism, and can been seen as embracing language offensive to people of other traditions. While the purpose of the prayer is to thank God for giving Israel the gift of *Shabbat*, it does it by means of belittling the other religious traditions of the world.

Interestingly the triumphalist and belittling wording is not universally found among different Jewish communities. Some Sephardic rites, for example, omit this text and instead includes *Yismihu* ("Those who keep the Sabbath"), a structurally similar prayer found in most versions of the *Musaf* (an additional service recited on the Sabbath). This precedent could support its replacement with the *Yismihu* prayer (following a Sephardic rite), which shares the same theme and is its structural equivalent in other versions of the *Amidah*.

While the *Aleinu* prayer concludes nearly every service in the Jewish year, attaining this position of honour during the Middle Ages, originally it was included only in the Rosh Hashanah *Musaf*. Its authorship has been ascribed variously to Rav, the men of the great assembly and to Joshua, though the true author is unknown. While the theme of the prayer focuses on the universal acceptance of God by all humanity, its first paragraph singles out the Jewish people (and its beliefs) as essentially different from the rest of humanity. "We must praise the Master of everything... who did not make us like the peoples of the earth, and did not place us like the families of the earth, and did not make our lot or our destiny like theirs."[141] It expresses sentiments far different from the universalistic hopes of the prayer's latter paragraphs.

Different as the *Aleinu's* triumphalist vision is from the pluralistic values of the twentieth-first century, the version found in *Sim Shalom* represents an edited version of an even more disturbing original. In medieval *siddurim* the phrases quoted above were followed by the following words: "They bow down to vanity and emptiness, and pray to a god who cannot save them" (Elbogen: 71). The line was seen as offensive by Christian authorities, poisoning already bad relations between Church and Synagogue (71).[142] While it was removed from most Ashkenazic *siddurim* as an act of censorship or self-censorship in the eighteenth century (Hoffman, 2002: 146-247) it has been reintroduced in many twentieth and twenty-first century Orthodox *siddurim*.[143] These lines were rendered particularly offensive, as it was

141 The translation included here that of the present author; the one included in *Sim Shalom* minimizes the negativity of the text by stating only, "God made our lot unlike that of other people, assigning us a unique destiny" (Reisner, 83). The rubric included at the bottom of the page in each edition of *Sim Shalom* ironically celebrates the universalistic hope of the prayer, while essentially ignoring the jarring triumphalism of the first paragraph.

142 Elbogen suggests that Christian offense was heightened when a Jewish apostate claimed that *v'rik* (and emptiness) referred to Jesus due to the similarity in the gamatria (numerical value) of word and name.

143 The sentence has been reintroduced in many modern Ashkenazic Orthodox *siddurim* and was never removed from most Sephardic versions of the prayer. See, for example, the versions of the *Aleinu* found in the Art Scroll series of *siddurim* or *Siddur Rinat Yisrael*.

(and in some communities still is) traditional to spit while reciting them.[144]

Though the most offensive language and actions are gone, the *Aleinu* still can be seen as denying the legitimacy of journeys other than our own, and can lead to sense of superiority and disrespect for the other peoples of the world. While the seventeenth century emendation can be seen as a precedent for further changes in the prayer, a more recent one can also be adduced. The Israeli 2009 *Masorti Siddur, Va'ani T'fillati*, omits "who did not make our lot or our destiny like theirs," and instead inserts the more positive "who gave us teachings of truth and planted within us eternal life." This language celebrates our history and tradition without belittling or minimizing the value of other truths or peoples.

Prayer is at the centre of the Jewish religious life. It is a constant of observance forming the structure for weekdays, Shabbat and Festivals. Its words, more than any others within our tradition, are recited and repeated again and again. Its messages, therefore, consciously and unconsciously shape our attitudes to ourselves, to our tradition, and to the rest of the world. Prayer, as the primary (or at least the most accessible) vehicle of the communication of religious values, also lends an aura of authenticity and "divine sanction," to its messages thus shaping the adherent to fit within the status quo. Because of its centrality to the Jewish experience our liturgy has grown and developed over the centuries. It has always responded to new ideas, and reflected changing understandings of God and the world. It is essential that this process continue, that our liturgy continues to speak with a voice, which teaches values of importance to us as Jews living in the modern world.

Rethinking our liturgy is also essential vis-à-vis our relationship with other communities, both Jewish and non-Jewish. Our liturgy is part of our public face; through which we communicate our values not only to our adherents, but also to the outside world. Our demand that other religious traditions (and internally other Jewish movements) accept our religious message as authentic, can only be strengthened and indeed be legitimate if we, through our words and prayers likewise accept the authenticity of their messages.

---

144 See. For example, http://e.yeshiva.org.il/ask/?id=4155, where the permissibility of spitting on the floor during the *Aleinu* in Chabad synagogues is examined.

We live in a world where traditional religious certainties and even the relevance of religion as a force for good is questioned. Indeed, our complex world with its multiplicity of religions and philosophies does not lend itself to simplistic statements of truth and falsehood. Absolute and triumphalist truth claims, therefore, have more often lent themselves to intolerance, oppression and violence, rather than to utopia. The Jewish embrace of pluralism – that there are multiple paths to the truth – is a challenge to this status quo. It is time that our liturgy and values speak with one voice; that the words of our mouths and the meditations of our hearts express the values that will allow our tradition to speak to the present and the future.

XI

The Challenge of Universality

THE TWENTY-FIRST CENTURY IS A TIME OF CHALLENGE FOR human society both local and global. Our mechanized society has transformed itself dramatically over the last one hundred years. On one hand transportation, communication, and access to knowledge have created a potential for a global village – almost millennial in character. On the other hand, our ability to kill has created devastation unheard of in history.

While the potential for a global society has never been better, the ability to see the other without fear or a rush to judgment has not been a marked characteristic of humanity either in this century or in any other. We have always sought universalisms such as the Golden Rule, or sought to universalize our particularities, to create most often an enforced uniformity, which denies the legitimacy of the other. Indeed, our rush to globalism is, hopefully, the last gasp of a modernist agenda which appears to view our western capitalistic society in terms seemingly connected with colonialism or social Darwinism (Spenserism), as the ideal to which the rest of the world should aspire or even be forced to conform. Yet, a world where a multiplicity of "truths" are seen as the norm would be a more "truthful" embrace of the realities of the human condition and the actuality of global society.

It is not surprising therefore that perhaps one of the most important unmet needs for both adults and children in our community is the teaching of empathy, appreciation and understanding of ethnic, racial, sexual, gender and religious differences. The failure to meet this need often leads to fear, hate and stereotyping of those who are different from us. The lack of understanding and appreciation for difference may also lead to violent acts and hate crimes, which are on the rise both in large urban areas, but also in smaller communities, in the United States, Canada and throughout the world.

Unfortunately, religions are not immune from the disease of drive for the universal, and the rush to judgment. Though they hope to communicate the words of God (or Gods) to their followers, often it is the words and prejudices that come out. My tradition, Judaism, unfortunately, is no different than other religions in this respect. Too often, we have vilified the other, and seen ourselves as "chosen" and therefore better. Like other religions, we have used our religion and God as an excuse to kill, and to look down on other people who are outside our tradition.

Rather than being seen as – and acting as an – instrument of peace, religion is perceived by many as the cause for much of the senseless hatred that characterizes human society both in the past and in the modern world. The crusades, inquisition, Arab – Israeli conflict, the Bosnia civil war and 9/11 – to name but a few of the world conflicts with roots or connections to religion – belie for many the idea that religion can serve a higher purpose, and can lead to human understanding and world peace.

Religion can be dangerous because, too often, its adherents make claims of the absolute truth. "We," they claim, "have the 'right and only answer' about the nature of the divine, and everyone else is wrong. We alone know what the divine wants for and from humanity." This truth claim often becomes at its mildest a push for conversion, and at its most extreme forced conversion, or even an excuse to kill, as it forms the basis for relations between those who follow the 'true and only revelation,' and those who do not. It also becomes the excuse for war as people use 'divine promises' as the basis for claims about land rights and national sovereignty.[145]

---

[145] It is my feeling that the mythological construct we call the divine transcends definition. Therefore when we take our own contingent notions of the divine and grant to them the attribution of truth we present a simulacra of "God(s)" to the world. Baudrillard, deconstructing classic semiotic theory, examined the use (and perhaps the breakdown in the use) of signs in the modern world, especially in the United States. He suggests that modern America (and I would read here world religions) is not interested in reality; rather, it is interested in the simulation of reality. Baudrillard denotes this false reality, which has no connection with, but which is taken to be reality, as hyperreality (Baudrillard,1994: 1). He asserts that hyperreality is used to ameliorate the crisis perceived as being inherent in reality and to manipulate the understanding of the addressed constituent groups – generally the masses, for which Baudrillard has a very low regard. Ultimately he predicts an infinite regression of signs referring only to other signs rather than to an empirical reality where all meaning is lost (4).

Beyond the Golden Rule

Rev. Charles Dodson, better known as Louis Carroll, in a fascinating poem called *the Hunting of the Snark* describes a quest to find a fantastic creature called a Snark. This poem, as all great literature, is open to many interpretations. It provides a useful analysis and critique of truth claims by religions, or indeed of any human institutions.

The hunt for the Snark can be understood as the search for universal truth, a quest that has engaged humankind since the dawn of time. The description of the crew resonates with the idea that all humanity – not just one culture, religion or civilization – has been engaged in this search.

> *The Crew was complete: it included a boots – A maker of bonnets and hoods – A barrister, brought to arrange their disputes – And a broker to value their goods. There was also a beaver, that paced on the deck, Or would sit making lace in the bow: And had often (the Bellman said) saved them from wreck, Though none of the sailors knew how* (Carroll: (http://www.literature.org/authors /carroll-lewis/the-hunting-of-the-snark/chapter-01.html).

These characters representing many stations and occupations represent the diversity of humanity. Yet, the poet realizes that though all humanity is engaged in the search for truth, there is not one road map to lead us on the correct path. Indeed, in truth, there is no map at all.

> *He had brought a large map representing the sea, without the least vestige of land: And the crew were much pleased when they found it to be A map they could all understand.*
>
> *"What's the good of Mercator's North Poles and Equators, Tropics, Zones, and Meridian Lines?" So the Bellman would cry: and the crew would reply "They are merely conventional signs."*
>
> *"Other maps are such shapes, with their islands and capes! But we've got our brave Captain to thank:"* (so the crew would protest) *"that he's brought us the best – A perfect and absolute blank!"* (http://www.literature.org/authors/carroll-lewis /the-hunting-of-the-snark/chapter-02.html).

The poem reminds us that the search for religious understanding of the world and the divine is not based on empirical observation, or logic. Rather, it is based on leaps of faith, which allow us to perceive the world in a different way. Religious claims cannot be proven by scientific method, and yet they still can help us to understand the universe and our place within it.[146]

The poet reminds us that this search is not without danger. For the Snark – the truth – that the crew seeks to find, may turn out to be a Boojum, a deadly creature, which can represent the illusion of absolute truth and certainty that leads to killing and persecution. Indeed, after a long search the crew fails to find a true Snark, and the last word of the poem are, "for the Snark was a Boojum you see." Dodson teaches that any time we believe that we know the final and absolute truth, and seek to impose it on others, than our truth is a 'boojum,' a deadly creature to be avoided at all costs.

Despite the dangers, human kind has been long sought out the "truth." Plato, Aristotle and other Greek philosophers – and subsequent philosophers, theologians and ethicist – have spent a great deal of time searching for universal truth. And the concept that this "truth" can one day be established – or already has been established – has become entrenched in ethics, religion, law and indeed in all aspects of human society.

Human beings want certainty, and become upset when they are confronted with the grey areas of human behavior and thought. Several years ago, while I was living in Glasgow, Scotland this human need was made clear in a series of small events. The kosher markets in Glasgow had stocked a number of products for Passover that had been produced in Israel, which included *kitniyot* (legumes which are forbidden for consumption on Passover by Ashkenazic but not many Sephardic authorities). The Glasgow Rabbinic Court (*Bet Din*) placed a notice in the paper stating that these products could only be eaten by Sefardim (Jewish communities that originated in Iberia), and not by the Ashkinazim (Jewish communities that originated in Central and eastern Europe) that comprised the majority of the community.

Interestingly, Jews from across the spectrum of observance from Reform to Orthodox (whatever their origin) were angered by the *Bet Din*'s

---

[146] Interestingly religion adopts a similar posture as science in regards to "truth claims." The modernist scientific model, drawing on Comte and others, posits the positivist idea that the "truth" can be established, and that scientific method is the best way to reach that goal. Scientific method is invested with the aura of "absolute truth". Religious thinkers replace scientific method with God concepts and other universals, which are also invested with the aura of "absolute truth."

action. They believed that the *Bet Din* brought Jewish Law into disrepute because it said that there were two different "right" answers concerning the *kashrut* of the products. They felt the uncertainty built into the rabbinic ruling undercut the entire system of Jewish law. What they failed to understand was that diversity of answers, as discussed above, in a real way, is the essence of the Jewish legal system.

They also failed to grasp, in a more global sense, that the idea that one small group, or even one universal culture or moral code has a lock on truth is replete with danger. If one is convinced that one is absolutely correct, then by definition everyone who does not agree is absolutely wrong – and therefore in need in some way of correction. And, if human history is any guide, the forms of correction that have been employed are violent indeed. This violence, perhaps, is the ultimate 'Boojam' in the search for truth.

Human history has been marked by the struggle nations and cultures seeking to impose their vision on the rest of the world. Religion, has often formed the basis of their belief that they have a lock on the truth. This is strikingly and ironically illustrated in Mark Twain's *War Prayer*. As a climax to the call to arms, both sides in the conflict cry out, "Bless our arms, grant us victory, O Lord our God, Father and Protector of our land and flag!" (Twain). In the world, as in the *War Prayer*, throughout history each side in most conflicts has been convinced that they own the "truth," that God is on their side and will lead them to victory.

One anthropological model of human society holds that human beings use the "other" as a means of strengthening self-identification. The "other" is often defined as profane or negative, while the defining society is seen as sacred and positive. The defining society is also seen as the possessor of "truth", while other societies possess either lesser truths, or out and out lies. The possession of "truth" and the stigmatization of the other strengthen the identity and legitimacy of the group. If, for example, one group claims that it has the true revelation from God, all those who accept this "truth" can be united in opposition to all those who do not accept it as true. Possession of the "truth" therefore is a unifying factor, because it sets the believers apart from the rest of humanity. Indeed, those who do not accept the truth can be labeled as heretics, infidels, or even less than human, and these labels can be used as an excuse to persecute, forcibly convert, or even to destroy those outside the group.

The conflicts attributed to exclusivist elements within our world society (which indeed are models themselves for universality) have led to a desire for a universal culture that would unite all humanity. How often has it been said that if we got rid of religion (for example) there would be peace in the world, or if everyone followed the Capitalist or Communist system then there would be world peace? It was long thought that answers such as these would solve the problems created by particularism. Even today, in the world of faith it is claimed that universal acceptance of spirituality, the Noachide laws or the Golden Rule will be the salvation of human society. Universalism is attractive, and the dangers posed by exclusive triumphalism have led philosophers and thinkers to look for universal truths that can unite everyone, and to do away with the small and large differences that lead to conflict.

Yet, a universal model of society is as dangerous as an exclusive triumphalist model, for one is but a global expansion of the other. Universalism is an attempt to impose one model of human behavior on the whole of humanity – to set aside the dangers of segmentary tribal society through the unity of the whole.

Universalism, in the guise of colonialism, has been used as an excuse for the enslavement of Africans both by Europeans and Muslims, and for the wholesale destruction of Aboriginal societies across the globe. The enforced Hellenism of the Selucids, the clash of Islamic and Christian society in the Middle Ages, and the cold and hot wars that between Communist and Capitalist societies – as well as the internal violence and repression found at times within both systems – in our own times are merely a few examples of the violence partially stemming from attempts to establish universal systems on human society.

Universalism is often violent both in its establishment, but also in its imposition. Universalism not only ignores differences, but also sees them as dangerous. Difference is seen as subversive because it undermines the general unity as people separate themselves from the "whole." How often in the Hebrew Bible and in history, has there been the refrain in societies attempting to impose themselves as universal, "There are people that are different..." (See, for example, Exodus 1:8-10; Esther 3:8; Daniel 3:8-12; and Daniel 6:6-10) leading to persecution, to a massacre or to a pogrom. In modern times the Stalinist purges in the U.S.S.R., the McCarthy era persecutions against people accused of being communist in the United States, and the residential schools here in Canada (and the United States) are examples of universalist societies persecuting those who did not fit the universalistic mode.

Rabbi Jonathan Sacks, in his insightful book *The Dignity of Difference*, interprets the story of the Tower of Babel as a rejection of enforced universalism (Sacks, 2002: 51-52). The universalistic society represented in the text claims that its unity and technology gives it the power of God. In their arrogance the people think that can control everything, and that they no longer are subjects of nature or even God. Rabbi Sacks teaches that the Torah rejects this model, and sees it as the ultimate hubris. Indeed, it is because of the tower builders' arrogance, that its building leads to the division of humanity into different nations speaking different languages.

In a similar vain, the Renascence Italian commentator Obadiah ben Jacob Sforno (1470-1550) also rejects universalism, and suggests that it was the real sin of the generation of the Tower. Sforno states that the real crime of the builders was that they tried to impose one religion on all of the people in the valley – within the Biblical myth this means all humanity. God dispersed the people so that each nation would individually participate in the search to understand the divine, and humanity's connection to it (Jacobson, 1958: 20).

Judaism, like all other religions must face this challenge for relevance in the creation of a peaceful human society. It is my own tradition, where I find a home, and it has provided me with answers and models as I search to find my place in our modern society. Yet, like many other faith traditions, it has many sides and interpretations. As such, along with the valuable, there are also issues, concepts and theologies that demand confrontation. As a monotheistic religion, it has long embraced truth claims, which have been used to delegitimize other religions and traditions. In ancient times this belief in absolute truth led to the destruction of temples to other gods and to the forcible conversion, at least in one case, of an entire people. Belief in the possession of absolute truth has led to an increasing disharmony within the Jewish community. Internally, truth claims have been used many times over the centuries – especially in our own times – to label entire sections of the community as inauthentic or even heretical. We have also not been immune to the dangers of seeing ourselves as better than other people because of our belief in our special access to the 'truth' and our 'unique' relationship with God. The concept of "chosen people," has led to a false sense of superiority and at times to an explicit bigotry against gentiles.

Traditional Jewish texts have even been misused, in the same way that the texts of other religions, as an excuse for terror and murder. Both Yigal Amir and Baruch Goldstein's actions, to name but two examples, have been justified by others based on texts from the Hebrew Bible. Indeed, some have even used Jewish texts to justify proposals for policies in the West Bank and Gaza that are little different than the ethnic cleansing that characterized the civil wars in Bosnia, Croatia and Serbia. While these voices, represent a small (but vocal) minority within today's Jewish community they cannot be ignored. Pretending they don't exist (in all of our faith expressions) merely creates a complacency that gives them power.

The challenge for the interfaith movement, for world religions, and indeed for human society as a whole, in the twenty-first century is to find a paradigm – or paradigms – which allows us to break both with absolute visions of exclusivity and universalism. We need to find a model that legitimizes the other, and realizes that truth can be found in many different guises. Indeed, if world religions cannot move beyond their claims of absolute truth, delegitimizing other traditions, then there may be no positive role for religion in the world of the future.

The challenge of acceptance, and surprisingly the fear of diversity also characterize the broader world of interfaith interaction. Easy answers and facile similarities are sought so that difference can be ignored and universality achieved. Narratives like the Golden Rule, which bring traditions together, are seen as answers to the complexities and the potential for conflict raised by difference. Yet, imposed universalism can be a form of violence, of imperialism and colonialism whether it is as broad as the imposition of a capitalistic free market system on a struggling third world country or as narrow as trying to impose (or find) a universal essential message – like the Golden Rule – on all the world's spiritual traditions.

XII

Journeys: A Tentative Theology

Spiritual Journeys[147]

> *Prayer often seems like a fruitless game of hide-and-seek where we seek and God hides…Yet I cannot leave prayer alone for long…I have a feeling that He has His own reasons for hiding Himself, and that finally all my seeking will prove infinitely worthwhile. And I am not sure what I mean by 'finding'. Some days my very seeking seems like a kind of 'finding'. And, of course, if 'finding' means the end of 'seeking', it is better to go on seeking. (Stern, 1975: 3-4)*

THIS MEDITATION, BY LESLIE WEATHERHEAD, HAS SPOKEN TO me ever since I first read it as a teenager in the Reform *siddur* (prayer book). Then as now, it has been a constant reminder to me that each of us is on a spiritual journey where we are seeking to find meaning and understand our place in the world. Sometimes vision and understanding seem so clear, but most often it is hard to see or find a sense of the divine. I am reminded of a joke, which describes a man who prayed for peace at the Western Wall in Jerusalem every day for 30 years. When asked how he felt, he replied, "on most days it feels like I am just praying to a wall."

I am often thankful that Judaism is not a creedal religion; that there is a constant space for me to search, grow and question.[148] There is a freedom that allows for every spiritual journey to have meaning, and for every generation – indeed every individual – to find its own theological and ontological answers. This liberty is found in the *Avot*, (Patriarchs) one of the central prayers of Jewish liturgy, according to an interpreta-

---

147 In this last section I attempt to place myself within my own context and examine my theology as it relates to the "other."

148 Judaism does not have a unitary creed, even within the particular denominations, rather it has a multiplicity of beliefs and theologies, none of which are considered to be the official and final statement of "truth."

tion attributed to the Ba'al Shem Tov (the eighteenth century founder of the Hasidic Movement). The prayer repetitiously calls upon the "God of Abraham," the "God of Isaac," and the "God of Jacob."[149] Why, the Ba'al Shem asks rhetorically, did it not just say, "God of our fathers"? His answer is instructive. Each generation of the past, present and future is on its own spiritual journey and has (will have) its own connection and understanding of the divine. All of these, he reminds us, are important and are reflections of the truth.

The Ba'al Shem Tov points to the realization that we can't live in the past, because our reality is in constant motion. Each of us is unique, made up of the desperate parts of our genetics, heritage and experiences. Indeed, we, ourselves, are changing from moment to moment as we move through our lives and face the contingencies that life brings us. My theology, therefore, is one of process and development, rather than of absolutes that remain frozen in time. It is built on and influenced by the past, my tradition and my experiences, but it is also shaped by who I am in the present. I called this section a tentative theology because I hope and trust that it will continue to change as I grow, learn, question and experience throughout the remainder of my life.

Theological reasoning in this respect is a form of myth, a structuring devise that helps to give meaning to the world and to my life. Its acceptance requires a leap of faith because it is not subject to proof. Myth, as Gillman points out, can remain meaningful even if it is clearly contradicted by scientific evidence (Gillman: 29). So, for example, I understand Genesis, Chapter One (the creation story) to demonstrate a sense of love and caring in and for the world and all that it contains, even though I accept evolution, and do not literally believe in the Biblical account. Indeed, my theological myth is built on my own idiosyncratic journey – with all its puzzle pieces – and by my search of my tradition for nuggets that help me to find my own relationship and understanding of the divine.

My spiritual journey is one of fits and starts, full of contradictions. My parents were a shaping force, yet my father is an atheist and secular Jew to this day. I am pulled by mystery, ritual and tradition, and yet attempt to define and see myself in a rational, indeed academic, manner. Inward mystical traditions call to me, and yet I see religion primarily in

---

149 When I pray, I choose to use a modern version which adds Sarah, Rebecca, Leah and Rachel.

terms of this world, as hopefully a force for transformation. I have had many teachers, with contradictory voices and from many traditions; all of whom have been pivotal is shaping who I am and where I am going.

The contradictions of my life are perhaps a reflection of the contradictions built into Judaism whose history renders all definitions difficult. Judaism is a culture, religious tradition, nation, and "genetic identity." At once it is all and none of these. Unlike many faith traditions Jewish identity is not necessarily primarily religious. It is possible, and indeed more and more likely, that a child can identify him or herself as Jewish without any religious content within their lives. Their Jewish identity is largely culturally constrained, or may be based on some connection with the State of Israel. Or indeed, it may be based solely on the possession of one or more Jewish parent.

During my early years (up until I was eleven) I grew up in just such a secular environment. Both my parents identified themselves as Jewish, but their connection was cultural with virtually no religious content. Passover and Hanukkah, the only holidays that we observed, were celebrated at the home of my grandparents – who themselves were socialists, with little or know connection to religious Judaism. Our only observance of the High Holidays was absence from school as my mother thought it would create issues for the other Jewish children if we attended.

At first glance my grandparents' observance of the Passover Seder was not a transcendent spiritual experience. My grandmother and her sisters would spend much of the time in the kitchen preparing the food, while my grandfather and the older men sat around a table chanting quickly in Hebrew. Meanwhile, all of the children were running wild throughout the house. Yet, the *Seder* ritual spoke in some way to my brothers and me. During the year, we would even play Seder using a Dixie cup holder as the ceremonial *kiddush* cup.

Within my parent's household while there was no sense of spirituality, there was, however, a liberal left-wing attitude that we could change the world. My parent's commitment was reflected in their support of civil rights, Eugene McCarthy, and rejection of the war in Vietnam. Their commitment and belief that we have the power and obligation to work to change the world has shaped my attitude to living the "religious" life.

As I reached the age of eleven our family began to attend the bar and bat mitzvah ceremonies of my cousins and other family friends. These synagogue services were the first that I had experienced. They were strange and foreign, and yet they engendered within me a curiosity to know more, and to connect with my religious tradition. This desire to know more of my heritage led me to Temple Israel, a Reform synagogue about a block from my parents home. Having worked in synagogue life for more than twenty years I know that it is not a regular occurrence for an eleven year old to walk into a synagogue asking for religious education, yet the principal and rabbi did not miss a beat, welcoming me to the community and allowing me to begin my Jewish journey in their Hebrew school. I don't know if they contacted my parents for the tuition, but I do know that they did not require my parents to join the synagogue for an additional two years when I began to prepare for my Bar Mitzvah. Their welcoming support helped me to quickly feel part of the community.

My parents strongly believed that each of their children had to make choices for their own lives. They encouraged us to think for ourselves, and were strongly supportive of any healthy interest that we had. They even were supportive if we made choices which were very different than their own. This freedom of thought was extremely important to me as I began to come into contact with the Jewish tradition. My father is still adamantly opposed to religion, seeing it as unscientific superstition. My mother, on the other hand, reconnected with the synagogue soon after me. Each member of my family follows, in this and many other matters, his or her own drummer.

Perhaps the two pivotal shaping influences of my teen years were two rabbis. One was Michael Robinson, the rabbi of Temple Israel, the other Chaim Potok, the author of *The Chosen* (a book depicting traditional Jewish life in Brooklyn in the 1940s). Rabbi Robinson's rabbinate was shaped by an all-encompassing commitment to social change. As a teacher and preacher he focused on the concept of *Tikkun Olam* (the repair of the world through acts of justice, righteousness and peace), and through his actions he lived all that he preached. In the Sixties he fought for civil rights, marching the Dr. King and participating in sit-ins and other peaceful protests. In the Seventies, he challenged us to fight against the war, and against the spread of nuclear weapons. He was throughout a peace activist demanding that we shed our prejudices and preconceived notions about every conflict, even one as close to home as that of Israel and the Palestinians. Rabbi Robinson's progressive views with his concurrent demand for activism resonated with the values of my parent's home, namely that we can and should work to create a better world. It shaped my belief that religion's primary goal is to build the kingdom of God here on earth as we work to effect real change and act as a force for transformation.

Chaim Potok spoke to me in a very different way. The world portrayed in *The Chosen* was very different than that of Temple Israel (a suburban Reform congregation). The book described the interaction between two young rabbinic students; one from the relatively acculturated world of American Jewish orthodoxy while the other was the son of a leader from a Hasidic sect (pietistic, mystically oriented Jews who resist assimilation into normative American life). Both worlds, Orthodox and Hasidic, were radically different from the modern Reform Judaism of Temple Israel. The book hinted at a richness of ancient texts, rituals and traditions largely absent in the rather staid observances of the Reform Movement (at least in the 70's). Potok led me to look for the mysterious and irrational within religion, where rituals and traditions help us to experience the sublime.

Both rabbis were instrumental in shaping my desire to enter the rabbinate. Michael Robinson exemplified the rabbi as "prophet", an agent for change leading people through the power of his message and actions. Potok portrayed deeply caring rabbis who were rooted in tradition and ritual with strong commitment to sharing their knowledge with their fellows. Both of these are models, which I attempt to emulate.

University years are a time of exploration and experimentation. Among other things, I used mine to discover who I was as a Jew. Each of the major movements had its attractions and had messages to teach me. Reform Judaism stressed the importance of autonomous decision making and social justice, Orthodox Judaism taught the importance of tradition and the regular observance of *mitzvot* (commandments) to create a life in constant relationship with God, and Conservative Judaism stressed the importance of a growing tradition where past and present come together to shape the future. (Conservative Judaism also stressed the importance of examining the Jewish tradition in a rigorous scholarly manner. This became very important to me as I studied at the Jewish Theological Seminary of America, the Conservative rabbinical school). Though often contradictory all of these voices shape me as both a rabbi and a Jew. At this stage in my life, I don't try to define myself by movement or affiliation. Rather I try to learn from all my many different teachers.

Learning and spiritual growth must be life long processes. In the Talmud, study and spiritual growth are described as being similar to swimming in the sea, no matter how far you swim there is always further to go. Over the years I have worked to keep learning and growing finding many teachers on the way. Some have been Jewish, but many have come from many differing belief systems.

From an Imam I learned of the many traditions and beliefs shared by Jew and Muslim – and yet tragically we can't find ways to get along. From a Jain priest I learned the story the seven blind men and the elephant, teaching me that the divine can be perceived in so many different ways, all of which are correct. From a rabbi I learned, *"Elu v'elu divarim elohim hayim"* (this answer and this answer are both the words of the living God), teaching me that there are no wrong answers so long as each of us works for the sake of heaven and not for our own power, prestige or egos. From a Wiccan elder I learned of the Wiccan Rede, and a strengthened belief in the consequences of our actions. From a Cree elder I learned of the spiritual connections realized when we hug a tree. Most recently, I learned from a puppy, the importance of living each day to its fullest no matter the difficulties and the shortness of time, and to approach every run in the park with a smile. Wherever I am, I go on looking for teachers.

My spiritual journey has taken me to places far from my parent's home. There have been many voices and many teachers. Some times my choices have horrified my parents as I veered away from their rational model and took on traditional practices and beliefs that they felt should long have been abandoned. Yet through it all, it is their voices that still shape me the strongest. I still believe that we have minds which were meant to be used, and that through our actions and our words that we can transform the world.

A Tentative Theology[150]

[The following theological statement is purely idiosyncratic. It represents a personal theology that underlies my own understanding of the divine and the relationship of human understanding to it. It is my mythological construct, which allows me to see and understand, in theo-

---

150 I have limited my theological discussion in this present context to those aspects germane to my thoughts about diversity and obligation for the world and for the "other".

logical terms, the simultaneous existence of contradictory beliefs all of which express truth about the divine.]

When I consider the nature of the divine, I am constantly reminded that I am a seeker, seeking an infinitely hiding ineffable God. The search is imbued with a fear that when ever I believe I am getting close to some epiphany or understanding that what I really will find is, in the words of the poet, a boojum, a deadly and dangerous simulacra that I, myself have created. It is for this reason that whenever I see or hear any attempt at a theological proof for God's existence, I feel like running away as quickly as possible. There are so many uncertainties, yet there are also so many visions of the divine, each fitting with a different time, place, and circumstance; all filling the needs of peoples looking for meaning and their place in the world. Even within my own tradition there are almost innumerable ways of understanding the divine, and our relation to Him, Her or It.

The Jain story of the elephant, each person experiencing a small part of the animal and believing it to be the whole, provides the lens of perspective reminding us that if there is a divine power, than it is beyond all human experience. Our attempts at definition are all descriptions of our experiences with the divine, which may not and cannot encompass the whole. I often think of the divine with the metaphor of a diamond with innumerable facets. We can only see one at a time, while others may experience a different one. The more voices that we hear, the more we can experience the true beauty of the diamond, or the true aspect of the elephant.

My single facet of the diamond is built the roots of my religious tradition, but I look to the mystic rather than the theologian or philosopher. Much like scientists the theologian and philosopher are dedicated to inferring God from logic and proofs – things that I cling to in my daily life. Yet, for me the divine is the stuff of myth – the language of mystic and prophet. The mystical myths and metaphors of Rabbi Isaac Luria (The Holy Ari, sixteenth century Safed), The Ba'al Shem Tov and Rabbi Shneur Zalman of Liadi (eighteenth century, Poland) speak far better about that which is beyond all empirical knowledge than all the logic of the *Guide for the Perplexed* (though there is much that is "mystical" in the guide.).

When we think of the divine in the terms of theology and philosophy we come up against all of the "omnis" – eternal, all-powerful, all-knowing, etc. These terms force us into proofs and logic – could, for example, an all-powerful god build a box that he/she could not open. They create an image of the divine that is removed from all contingency and contextuality; an image of God that is fixed and without apology. To me this form of theology is an expression of arrogance, as if we claim the power and knowledge to place God into a box. In Buber's terms, when we move beyond the experience of relationship, and attempt at knowledge and definition we objectify the divine. The mystic, on the other hand realizes that we can never truly "know" the divine, all we have is our limited human perspective and our own experiences.

My mystical myth begins with a statement I recall, that was attributed to the Ba'al Shem Tov. He called upon us to open our eyes, because everywhere we look we would see that bushes were burning, but not being consumed. At first glance, this text is a reminder that small and large miracles are happening all around us, yet we walk through the world and fail to see them. But, within the context of Hasidic theology, it is saying much more. We walk through the world and we see materiality. We see the objects we have constructed, plants, animals and other people and each appears to be separate and discrete. Yet, with a mystical eye, we have the opportunity to see God's presence and being within everything. To the mystic, everything on one level is separate but on another level there is a unity to all existence, and that unity and much beyond it is the divine.[151]

To a mystic God's all encompassing presence is set forth in the Torah, "Know this day and set it upon your heart that the Eternal is Lord…there is none else" (Deuteronomy 4:39). The Hasid reads the last two words, as "there is nothing else." Everything is God, though we don't always see it. The divine essence is constantly in moving towards a state of *hitlabbeshut* (clothing itself in materiality). This garbing acts both as a means of hiding the divine, but also contradictorily revealing it.

As I consider this mythic vision of the world, it challenges me because it brings, to some extent my worlds of interpretation together. The mystic seems to intuit, that which physics has demonstrated. To the scientist, while we, and the material objects around us, seem solid, yet they are made up of multitudes of elementary particles that are in constant motion. Indeed, quantum physics challenges our notions of time and space as a particle can be in two places simultaneously. We seem different

---

151 The idea that the world and everything in it is God is denoted by the theological term pantheism. The Chasidic concept is an expression of panentheism – that God encompasses all the world, but also extends beyond it.

and discrete, yet the stars and we are composed of the same basic materials, and are tied together in ways we cannot understand.

The mystic Isaac Luria building on kabbalistic concepts found in the Zohar created a complex myth on the nature of the creation and the divine. This myth drew heavily on the theme of exile, both of God from the world, and indeed aspects of God from God's essence. In primordial time, the Ari posits, the *Ein Sof* (the ineffable, unknowable, unconceivable God) was everywhere – and perhaps nowhere. There was no room for anything else. The *Ein Sof*, therefore, initiated a process of contraction (*tzimtzum*) in order to make room for the creation of the universe. This contraction was followed by a process of emanation from the *Ein Sof*, moving, in essence, from the unknowable to the more knowable imminent aspects of the divine.

While the Lurianic mystical myth became one of the dominant trends in Jewish mysticism until the present, it was not accepted without reinterpretation within the Hasidic mystical tradition. The concept of *tzimtum* was considered to be especially troubling, as it implied the essential absence of God from the world. The Hasidim, on the other hand believed that no place was free from the divine presence. Yet, how can one interpret contraction - *tzimtzum* - if God is everywhere, and everything is God? To the Hasid, *tzimtzum* became a matter of perspective. From our perspective we experience "every-thing", that is to say materiality and the apparent absence of the divine. From God's perspective, however, there is no absence, there is "no-thing" no true differentiation only God.

Within the Hasidic reinterpretation of the Lurianic myth emanation becomes a process of moving both from the unknowable (immaterial) to the knowable (material), but also from the one to the many. From the *Ein Sof's* perspective there is only God, there is still pure unity. From our perspective there is the diversity of creation. The challenge that we face is to see the essential unity of all existence; to see the divine essence that underlies all that we normally perceive as merely mundane and material.

For the Hasid there is a definite level of valuation between the knowable and the unknowable. The material world of *gashmiut*, or corporeality is considered a mask that prevents us from seeing the unknowable unity of *ruchniut*, or spirit. Despite this, however, since the divine is in everything even in materiality, we can serve in every aspect of our lives. Just like sacred activities, all mundane activities – everything we do –

awaits and invites elevation, achieved through the realization that the divine is hidden within it. Eating, drinking, singing, dancing and even sexual intercourse all can be, and should be, holy activities. The Hasidic world view does not require a withdrawal from the world or from other people, but rather it demands that we seek to make everyday and every moment an opportunity of elevation.

In my understanding of the myth I move even further away from the negative valuation of this world. I see the process of emanation not as the creation of a materiality that masks or prevents the true essence, which is God; instead, I envision a process of revelation where the divine is made known in the world. The divine is perceived, not only as the underlying essence, which expresses unity, but also in the truth of the world's materiality and diversity and our interconnectivity to it – that is to say through the beauty of many different flowers and plants or the comfort of a hug. The rabbis speak of this diversity in the midrashic analysis of creation. The text points to the difference between the divine and a human king. When a king mints coins with his image, the image on each coin is identical, but when the divine mints human beings, all in the divine image, each male and female is unique. Our diversity, and indeed all diversity is a revelation of the divine. It is not, however, just humanity that is in image of God, rather it is the entire diversity of creation.

The myth provides us with an understanding of the divine that is simultaneously imminent and transcendent. Here again the difference is perspective. For some, the material clothing of the divine essence can render vision opaque leading to a feeling that the divine is not present in the world. Some, feeling a sense of despair or existential loneliness may come to the same conclusion. Some, accepting the transcendence of the divine, may see the wonders of creation, and rejoice in the creative power of the divine, but see it as separate from creation. Others, however, may pierce beyond the material seeing something akin to the essence itself, and this indeed is the goal of this mystical system, allowing us to feel the imminence of the divine presence in everything we see, feel and experience.

Yet, our search often is to understand that aspect of the divine that is beyond the material. We search for the essence of the divine, which to me is ultimately no-thing. It is unknowable and indefinable. It is all around us in everything, and we are challenged to open our eyes and to experience it. This vision of the world gives tremendous importance to perspective, based as it is on the realization that all human understanding is contingent and contextual. Perspective limits what we can see, experience, and understand. Therefore, understandings we have of the divine, based on our unique perspectives, are true but not the entire truth, which to the Hasid and to me is impossible to encompass. The words and expressions we use, whether "god", "gods", or "no god" enable us to connect, and to describe what we experience. Whether similar or contradictory all are "truth." The Jain elephant is much more than a leg, or tail each experienced by a different blind man. So too, the divine is much more than tree, plant, person or even image from a particular tradition – each are an important part that together helps us to gain a small glimpse of that which is ultimately beyond definition or cognition.

These realizations lead me to a rejection of a common misreading of Darwin's view of evolution. Some misread Darwin, finding a set trajectory identifying humanity as the goal of evolution. This misreading has shaped not only how humans look at themselves and their culture, but also how they look at the rest of the world. It creates an idea of progress that has justified a theory of manifest destiny utilized in the conquest of "less developed peoples." Darwin's theory of survival of the fittest in actuality has no goal, but only a beginning leading to many branches. Therefore within the scope of culture all theologies and perspectives are on an equal footing, each allowing diverse peoples to respond to and reach out for an understanding of the divine. This leads me to reject views that look at theology as a progression of ideas from the less sophisticated polytheism to the more sophisticated monotheism.[152] This concept of theological progression is ethnocentric denying the validity of theological expressions from across the globe. It is also dangerous, because that denial can be used as an excuse for missionization, and the subsequent destruction of a distinct culture and tradition. It also prevents us from learning about and appreciating another facet expressing the human search for the divine.

The understanding that all is God and "there is nothing else." Leads, perforce, to a sense of obligation towards all creation. As examined earlier, if every human, and indeed everything on this earth, is interconnected and is a revelation of the divine, this creates a great responsibility, on us. Unique, among all that is part of this ongoing revelation, we are both self aware and powerful. No other creature on earth can shape the

---

152 See, for example, Arthur Green, *Radical Judaism*. (New Haven: Yale University Press, 2010) p. 28.

environment for the good or ill of all creation. No other creature has the power to drive whole species to extinction. This power gives us the obligation to care, as best we can, for the entirety of creation. Because when we destroy another human, another species, or indeed the environment we are destroying an aspect of the revelation of the divine.

This responsibility is reflected in Judaism by the concept that we are all *shutafim* (partners) with God in creation and the realization of revelation. God, according to this tradition, did not finish the work of creation, but rather left it to be completed by humanity. This can be seen in the rite of circumcision, where the male baby, born in the way that God intended he should be born, only enters the covenant after his parents observe this ritual. We, therefore, are commanded not to wait for God to perfect the world but rather have the obligation to at least begin the work ourselves.

The tradition uses the concept of *imitatio dei* to impel us to this responsibility. Each day in the morning service we read Psalm 146, which reminds us that God loves all the aspects of the divine revelation. Therefore God takes care of all the disadvantaged of society. This psalm is a call, reminding us that it is we, as God's partners that share in this responsibility.

Even the concept of the coming of the messiah or, more comfortably for me, the messianic age – a final redemption of the word – is not left only to God, but rather to human action. A Talmudic legend (Sanhedrin 98a) recounts that Rabbi Joshua ben Levi once asked of the messiah (notably sitting at the gates of Rome with the beggars and lepers) when he would come? The Messiah responded "today." When the messianic age failed to come, Rabbi Joshua asked Elijah the Prophet what the messiah had meant. Elijah explained that the messiah was quoting psalms, "Today, if you harken to my voice." A Hasidic rabbi, building on this text taught, "Why did the messiah not come today or yesterday, it is because we were the same today as we were yesterday.[153]

This sense of human partnership with God is taken up in mystical sources. The kabbalistic mystical myth presents a very different image of the divine than the "omni God" who is beyond all need and connection to (or need of) humanity and the world. To the kabbalist God needs us, just as we need God. As alluded to above, the Zohar and other mystical

---

[153] Martin Buber reported that his grandfather, a Hasid, in answering why the messiah did not come, told a young Buber that the messiah was waiting for him. (Moore, 1996:276)

texts posit a process of emanation from an unknowable *Ein Sof* leading to the revelation of more and more knowable aspects of the divine, known as the ten *sefirot*. In a sense these are hypostasis of the attributes of action through which we perceive God's activities in our world. There are, for example, *sefirot* called Justice (*Din*) and Righteousness (*Hesed*). To the kabbalist these *sefirot* are not static but rather are part of a dynamic interaction, which when harmonious, facilitates the flow of energy from the *Ein Sof* to the material world. It is here that human action plays a central role. Our observance of the commandments creates energy, which flows upwards, facilitating the harmony in the supernal realms that enables the energy to flow down and vivify the world. This mutual reliance creates a sense of partnership between humanity and the divine.

This concept of partnership is expanded in the Lurianic recreation of the kabbalistic myth. Luria, building on his focus on exile, suggests a catastrophic climax, due to a primordial sin or imbalance, to the process of emanation. The seven lower *sefirot*, referred to as the luminous vessels, shatter leading to the spread of the sparks of the divine being spread across the universe. To Luria these sparks of the divine were in exile from the supernal realms and the Ein Sof. Within this new mystical myth the human role, and the interdependence of the divine and humanity is expanded as the divine sparks are lifted and returned to God only through human action, referred to as *Tikkun Olam* repair of the world.

While Hasidic mystics, working for consistency in their mystical narrative, see this myth as a metaphor of human perspective (that to us the essence of the divine found underlying everything appears as a multiplicity spread across the globe, but not so to the divine where all appears as a unity), to me, I find in its language a greater sense of connection, relationship, mutuality and obligation. What we do matters, and not only to ourselves. The myth adds a level of importance to what we do, and how we look at the world. As partners of the divine, indeed as necessary partners, it is up to us to transform the world, the raise the sparks back to their source, and as we do so, we repair not only the earth, but the divine itself.

About the Author

RABBI DAVID A. KUNIN GRADUATED FROM BRANDEIS UNIVERSITY with a degree in Medieval History and then attended the Jewish Theological Seminary of America, where he was ordained as a Rabbi and received an MA in Judaic Studies. He has served as rabbi internationally from Glasgow to Elmira, San Diego and Edmonton. He now is the spiritual leader of the Jewish Community of Japan.

Rabbi Kunin is committed to Jewish learning and to a strong laity that play a central role in the religious leadership of the congregation. He believes that Jewish learning and growth is a life-long process. He also believes that spiritual growth, as we build our relationship with the community and God should be a continuous part of Jewish life.

He believes in the importance of harmonious relations between people from diverse religious communities. Interfaith relations have therefore been a continuous mark of his rabbinate. He served as the Chair of the Southern Tier Interfaith Coalition (Elmira, NY), where he created the Walking Together program, and was long time board member and president of the Edmonton Interfaith Centre for Education and Action. He also served on the Academic Senate of St. Stephen's College and the Advisory Board of the Chester Ronning Centre for the Study of Religion in Public Life. David also served for ten years as the Jewish Chaplain at the University of Alberta.

He is a recipient of the Alberta Centennial Medal and the 2013 Interfaith Center Award for Excellence in Interfaith Leadership both in recognition of his community work.

He was also honored by the City of Edmonton for leadership and service to the community. David was also named a Global National TV "Everyday Hero" in 2008 for his work in bringing diverse communities together.

Rabbi Kunin speaks widely on Jewish history, mysticism and Israel and on issues of understanding between religious traditions. In his spare time he enjoys photography, hiking and skiing.

Bibliography

Abbott, Lyman. "Religion Essentially Characteristic of Humanity." In *The Dawn of Religious Pluralism: Voices from the World's Parliament of Religions, 1893*, by Richard Hughes. Seager. La Salle, IL: Open Court, 1993.

Ariarajah, Wesley S. *Not Without My Neighbour: Issues in Interfaith Relations*. Geneva: WCC Publications, 1999.

"Arizona Interfaith Movement." Arizona Interfaith Movement. Accessed July 17, 2013. http://www.azifm.org/interfaith-news/many-people-many-faiths-one-common-principle-the-golden-rule-overview/.

"Arizona Interfaith Movement." Arizona Interfaith Movement. Accessed July 18, 2013. http://www.interfaitharizona.com/.

Bartens, Hans. "The Postmodern Weltanschauung and Its Relation to Modernism." In *A Postmodern Reader*, by Joseph P. Natoli and Linda Hutcheon. Albany: State University of New York Press, 1993.

Baudrillard, Jean. *Simulacra and Simulation*. Ann Arbor: University of Michigan Press, 1994.

Bauman, Zygmunt. "Postmodernity, or Living with Ambivalence." In *Modernity and Ambivalence*. Ithaca, NY: Cornell University Press, 1991.

Bayfield, Tony, and Marcus Braybrooke. "Making Theological Space." In *Dialogue with a Difference: The Manor House Group Experience*. London: SCM Press, 1992.

Berkowitz, Henry. "The Voice of the Mother of Religions on the Social Questions." In *The Dawn of Religious Pluralism: Voices from the World's Parliament of Religions, 1893*, by Richard Hughes. Seager. La Salle, IL: Open Court, 1993.

Bonney, Charles C. "Words of Welcome." In *The Dawn of Religious Pluralism: Voices from the World's Parliament of Religions, 1893*, by Richard Hughes. Seager. La Salle, IL: Open Court, 1993.

Boyarin, Daniel. *Border Lines: The Partition of Judaeo-Christianity*. Philadelphia, PA: University of Pennsylvania Press, 2004.

Braybrooke, Marcus. *Interfaith Organizations 1893-1979: A Historical Directory*. New York: Edward Mellon Press, 1983.

Buber, Martin, and Walter Arnold Kaufmann. *I and Thou*. New York: Charles Scribner's Sons, 1970.

Burris, John P. *Exhibiting Religion: Colonialism and Spectacle at International Expositions, 1851-1893*. Charlottesville: University Press of Virginia, 2001.

Burrows, John H. "Words of Welcome." In *The Dawn of Religious Pluralism: Voices from the World's Parliament of Religions, 1893*, by Richard Hughes. Seager. La Salle, IL: Open Court, 1993.

Cohen, Shaye J. D. *Why Aren't Jewish Women Circumcised?: Gender and Covenant in Judaism*. Berkeley: University of California Press, 2005.

Cook, Joseph. "Strategic Certainties of Comparative Religion." In *The Dawn of Religious Pluralism: Voices from the World's Parliament of Religions, 1893*, by Richard Hughes. Seager. La Salle, IL: Open Court, 1993.

Cornille, C. *Criteria of Discernment in Interreligious Dialogue*. Eugene, Or.: Cascade Books, 2009.

Derrida, Jacques. "Structure, SIgn and Play in the Discourse of Human Science." In *A Postmodern Reader*, by Joseph P. Natoli and Linda Hutcheon. Albany: State University of New York Press, 1993.

"Designated Sacred Space Project." Multifaith Saskatchewan. Accessed July 18, 2013. http://www.multifaithsask.org/designated-sacred-space-project-2/.

Dorff, Elliot. "Use of a Synagogue by a Christian Group." In *Responsa, 1980-1990: [She'elot U-teshuvot]*, by David J. Fine. New York: Rabbinical Assembly, 2005.

Dubuisson, Daniel. "Exporting the Local: Recent Perspectives on 'Religion' as a Cultural Catagory." *Religion Compass* 1, no. 6 (2007).

"Edmonton Interfaith Centre for Education and Action." Edmonton Interfaith Centre for Education and Action. Accessed July 17, 2013. http://www.edminterfaithcentre.ca/?page_id=31.

Elbogen, Ismar. *Jewish Liturgy: A Comprehensive History*. Philadelphia: Jewish Publication Society, 1993.

Frew, Don. "Unpublished Remarks, Nain Connect Meeting in Phoenix, AZ." E-mail message to author. July 2011.

Frishman, Elyse D. *Mishkan T'filah: A Reform Siddur : Services for Shabbat*. New York: Central Conference of American Rabbis, 2007.

Gensler, Harry. "The Golden Rule." The Golden Rule. 2012. Accessed July 18, 2013. http://www.harryhiker.com/goldrule.htm.

Gibbons, James. "The Needs of Humanity Supplied by the Catholic Religion." In *The Dawn of Religious Pluralism: Voices from the World's Parliament of Religions, 1893*, by Richard Hughes. Seager. La Salle, IL: Open Court, 1993.

Gillman, Neil. *The Death of Death: Resurrection and Immortality in Jewish Thought*. Woodstock, VT: Jewish Lights, 1997.

Gitlitz, David M. *Secrecy and Deceit: The Religion of the Crypto-Jews*. Albuquerque: University of New Mexico, 2002.

Gmeiner, John. "Union of the Human Race." In *The Dawn of Religious Pluralism: Voices from the World's Parliament of Religions, 1893*, by Richard Hughes. Seager. La Salle, IL: Open Court, 1993.

Goldberg, Monique Susskind., Diana Villa, David Golinkin, and Israel Warman. *Ask the Rabbi: Women Rabbis Respond to Modern Halakhic Questions*. Jerusalem: Schechter Institute of Jewish Studies, 2010.

"The Golden Rule." Wikipedia. November 07, 2013. Accessed July 18, 2013. http://en.wikipedia.org/wiki/The_Golden_Rule.

Gordis, Daniel. *God Was Not in the Fire: The Search for a Spiritual Judaism*. New York: Scribner, 1995.

Green, Arthur. *Radical Judaism: Rethinking God and Tradition*. New Haven: Conn.: Yale University Press, 2010.

Grim, John A. "The Forum on Religion and Ecology at Yale." Indigenous. 1998. Accessed July 18, 2013. http://fore.research.yale.edu/religion/indigenous/.

Heschel, Abraham Joshua, and Samuel H. Dresner. *I Asked for Wonder: A Spiritual Anthology*. New York: Crossroad, 1983.

Higginson, Thomas W. "The Sympathy of Religions." In *The Dawn of Religious Pluralism: Voices from the World's Parliament of Religions, 1893*, by Richard Hughes. Seager. La Salle, IL: Open Court, 1993.

Hirai (Kinza Riuge M. Hirai), Ryuge K. "The Real Position of Japan Towards Christianity." In *The Dawn of Religious Pluralism: Voices from the World's Parliament of Religions, 1893*, by Richard Hughes. Seager. La Salle, IL: Open Court, 1993.

Hirsch, Emile. "Universal Religion." In *The Dawn of Religious Pluralism: Voices from the World's Parliament of Religions, 1893*, by Richard Hughes. Seager. La Salle, IL: Open Court, 1993.

Hitchens, Christopher. *God Is Not Great: How Religion Poisons Everything*. Toronto: Emblem, 2007.

Hoffman, Lawrence A., and Marc Zvi. Brettler. *The Amidah*. Woodstock, VT: Jewish Lights Pub., 1998.

Hoffman, Lawrence A., and Marc Zvi. Brettler. *Tachanun and Concluding Prayers*. Woodstock, VT: Jewish Lights Pub., 2002.

Hordes, Stanley M. *To the End of the Earth: A History of the Crypto-Jews of New Mexico*. New York: Columbia University Press, 2005.

"The Hunting of the Snark." Literature.org. Accessed July 18, 2013. http://www.literature.org/authors/carroll-lewis/the-hunting-of-the-snark/chapter-01.html.

Jacobson, Isaschar. *Iyunim Be-farahiyot Ha-Torah Al Pi Ha-sifrut Ha-parshanit*. Tel Aviv: Sinai, 1958.

"Jain World." Jain World. Accessed July 18, 2013. http://www.jainworld.com/education/stories25.asp.

Jibara, Christophore. "A Voice from Syria." In *The Dawn of Religious Pluralism: Voices from the World's Parliament of Religions, 1893*, by Richard Hughes. Seager. La Salle, IL: Open Court, 1993.

Justin, and Michael Slusser. *Dialogue with Trypho*. Washington, D.C.: Catholic University of America Press, 2003.

Kant, Immanuel. "Fundamental Principles of the Metaphysics of Morals." 2004. Accessed July 17, 2013. http://philosophy.eserver.org/kant/metaphys-of-morals.txt.

Kishimoto, Nobuto. "Religion in Japan." In *The World's Parliament of Religions*, by John Henry Burrows. 2010.

Kol Haneshamah: Shabbat Vehagim. Wyncote, PA: Reconstructionist Press, 1996.

Küng, Hans. *Judaism*. London: SCM Press, 1992.

Küng, Hans. "DECLARATION OF A GLOBAL ETHIC." DECLARATION OF A GLOBAL ETHIC. Accessed July 17, 2013. http://www.religioustolerance.org/parliame.htm.

Kunin, David A. "May the Words of Our Mouths Be Acceptable: Rethinking Triumphalist and Rejectionist Prayers in the Siddur." *Conservative Judaism*, 2013.

Kunin, David A. "Multifaith: New Directions." *Journal of Ecumenical Studies*, 2012.

Kunin, Seth D. "Juggling Identities among the Crypto-Jews of the American Southwest." *Religion* 31, no. 1 (2001): 41-61.

Kunin, Seth Daniel. *Religion: The Modern Theories*. Baltimore: Johns Hopkins University Press, 2003.

Lewy, Yochanan, Alexander Altmann, Yiẓḥak Heinemann, Philo, Sa'adia Ben Joseph, and Judah Halevi. *Three Jewish Philosophers*. New York: Atheneum, 1969.

Long, Jefferey D. *Jainism: An Introduction*. London: I.B. Tauris, 2009.

Lévi-Strauss, Claude. *The Savage Mind*. [Chicago]: University of Chicago Press, 1966.

Lyotard, Francois. "Excerpts from the Postmodern Condition: A Report on Knowledge." In *A Postmodern Reader*, by Joseph P. Natoli and Linda Hutcheon. Albany: State University of New York Press, 1993.

Masuzawa, Tomoko. *The Invention of World Religions, Or, How European Universalism Was Preserved in the Language of Pluralism*. Chicago: University of Chicago Press, 2005.

Melville, Herman. *Moby Dick*. 1967.

Moore, Daniel J. *Martin Buber: Prophet of Religious Secularism*. New York: Fordham Press, 1996.

Mullick, Sunrit. "Protap Chandra Majumdar and Swami Vivekananda at the Parliament of Religions: Two Interpretations of Hinduism and Universal Religion." In *A Museum of Faiths: Histories and Legacies of the 1893 World's Parliament of Religions*, by Eric J. Ziolkowski. Atlanta, GA: Scholars Press, 1993.

Natoli, Joseph P., and Linda Hutcheon. *A Postmodern Reader*. Albany: State University of New York Press, 1993.

Neely, Alan. "The Parliament of the World's Religions: 1893 and 1993." *International Bulletin of Missionary Research* 18:2, no. 60.

New Seminary. "The New Seminary for Interfaith Studies." The New Seminary. Accessed July 18, 2013. http://www.newseminary.org/.

Newman, Louis I. *The Hasidic Anthology*. New York: Schocken Books, 1975.

Panikkar, Raimon. *The Intra-religious Dialogue*. New York (N.Y.): Paulist Press, 1999.

Philo, Ben Joseph Sa'adia, Judah, Yochanan Lewy, Alexander Altmann, and Yiẓḥak Heinemann. *Three Jewish Philosophers*. New York: Atheneum, 1969.

"The Platinum Rule - A Golden Rule Upgrade." Wisdom Website RSS. Accessed July 18, 2013. http://wisdomwebsite.com/the-platinum-rule-a-golden-rule-upgrade/.

Plaut, W. Gunther. *The Growth of Reform Judaism; American and European Sources until 1948.* New York: World Union for Progressive Judaism, 1965.

Reisner, Avram Israel. *Siddur Sim Shalom for Weekdays.* New York: Rabbinical Assembly, 2002.

Rollins, Peter (2008). *How (Not) to Speak About God* Kindle DX version. Retrieved from Amazon.com

Roth, Joel. *The Halakhic Process: A Systemic Analysis.* New York: Jewish Theological Seminary of America, 1986.

Sacks, Jonathan. *The Dignity of Difference: How to Avoid the Clash of Civilizations.* London: Continuum, 2002.

"Scarboro Golden Rule Movie Screened at United Nations | NAINews." NAINews. Accessed July 18, 2013. http://nainblog.wordpress.com/2011/03/28/scarboro-golden-rule-movie-screened-at-united-nations/.

"Scarboro Missions." Scarboro Missions — A Society of Canadian Catholics, Priests, and Laity Dedicated to the Mission of Jesus Christ. 2000. Accessed July 18, 2013. http://www.scarboromissions.ca/golden_rule/index.php.

Seager, Richard Hughes. *The Dawn of Religious Pluralism: Voices from the World's Parliament of Religions, 1893.* La Salle, IL: Open Court, 1993.

Seager, Richard Hughes. *The World's Parliament of Religions: The East/West Encounter, Chicago, 1893.* Bloomington: Indiana University Press, 2009.

Shaw, George Bernard. *Man and Superman.* Press: University, 1999. Accessed July 18, 2013. www.bartleby.com/157/6.html.

Sidgwick, Henry. *The Methods of Ethics.* [Chicago]: University of Chicago Press, 1962.

Singer, Marcus G. "The Golden Rule." *Philosophy* 38, no. 146 (1963): 293.

Soloveitchik, Joseph B. "Confrontation." Confrontation. Accessed July 18, 2013. http://www.bc.edu/dam/files/research_sites/cjl/texts/cjrelations/resources/articles/soloveitchik/.

Soloveitchik, Joseph Dov., and Netan'el Helfgoṭ. *Community, Covenant, and Commitment: Selected Letters and Communications of Rabbi Joseph B. Soloveitchik.* Jersey City: Published for the Toras HoRav Foundation by Ktav Publishing House, 2005.

Soyer, Shaku. "Arbitration Instead of War." In *The Dawn of Religious Pluralism: Voices from the World's Parliament of Religions, 1893*, by Richard Hughes. Seager. La Salle, IL: Open Court, 1993.

Sperber, Daniel. "IJII." How Not to Make Halakhic Rulings. 2009. Accessed July 18, 2013. http://www.jewishideas.org/articles/how-not-make-halakhic-rulings.

Stern, Chaim, ed. *Gates of Prayer*. New York: Central Conference of American Rabbis, 1975.

Swindler, Leonard. "Understanding Dialogue." *Journal of Ecumenical Studies* 43, no. 2 (2008).

Tcheraz, Minas. "The Armenian Church." In *The Dawn of Religious Pluralism: Voices from the World's Parliament of Religions, 1893*, by Richard Hughes. Seager. La Salle, IL: Open Court, 1993.

Twain, Mark. "THE WAR PRAYER." Accessed July 18, 2013. http://lexrex.com/informed/otherdocuments/warprayer.htm.

The Union Prayerbook for Jewish Worship. New York: Central Conference of American Rabbis, 1961.

"Versions of the Golden Rule in 21 World Religions." Versions of the Golden Rule in 21 World Religions. Accessed July 18, 2013. http://www.religioustolerance.org/reciproc.htm.

Vidal, C. "Wat Is Een Wereldbeeld? (What Is a Worldview?)." In *Nieuwheid Denken. De Wetenschappen En Het Creatieve Aspect Van De Werkelijkheid*, edited by H. Van Belle and J. Van Der Veken. Leuven: Acco, 2008. Accessed July 18, 2013. http://cogprints.org/6094/2/Vidal_2008-what-is-a-worldview.pdf.

Vivekananda. "Hinduism." In *The Dawn of Religious Pluralism: Voices from the World's Parliament of Religions, 1893*, by Richard Hughes. Seager. La Salle, IL: Open Court, 1993.

Wattles, Jeffrey. *The Golden Rule*. New York: Oxford University Press, 1996.

Webb, Mohammed. "The Spirit of Islam." In *The Dawn of Religious Pluralism: Voices from the World's Parliament of Religions, 1893*, by Richard Hughes. Seager. La Salle, IL: Open Court, 1993.

"William E. Cameron." William E. Cameron. Accessed July 17, 2013. http://www.nga.org/cms/home/governors/past-governors-bios/page_virginia/col2-content/main-content-list/title_cameron_william.html.

Williams, Fannie B. "What Can Religion Further Do to Advance the Condition of the American Negro." In *The Dawn of Religious Pluralism: Voices from the World's Parliament of Religions, 1893*, by Richard Hughes. Seager. La Salle, IL: Open Court, 1993.

Wilson, Shawn. *Research Is Ceremony: Indigenous Research Methods*. Black Point, N.S.: Fernwood Pub., 2008.

"World Parliament of Religions (1893)." World Parliament of Religions, 1893 (Boston Collaborative Encyclopedia of Western Theology). Accessed July 17, 2013. http://people.bu.edu/wwildman/bce/worldparliamentofreligions1893.htm.

"www.israelinsider.com / Servermaintenance." www.israelinsider.com / Servermaintenance. Accessed July 18, 2013. http://israelinsider.com/articles/deplomacy/11640.htm.

Yu, Pung Kwang. "Confucianism." In *The World's Parliament of Religions: The East/West Encounter, Chicago, 1893*, by John Henry Burrows. 2101.

Ziolkowski, Eric Jozef. *A Museum of Faiths: Histories and Legacies of the 1893 World's Parliament of Religions*. Atlanta, GA: Scholars Press, 1993.

Index

Abbott, Lyman 22
aboriginal rights 32
Abrahamic and non-Abrahamic faiths
 79
Abrahamic faiths 78-79, 122, 124
absolute truth 62, 71, 98, 100, 121,
  126, 140, 142, 145
  rabbinic rejection 65-69
African Americans 17, 30
Age of Enlightenment 37
ahimsa (non-violence) 73, 74
Akiba, Rabbi 36, 51, 54-55, 58
Aleinu 131, 135
American self-identity 18
American values 116
  epitome of human values 117
Amidah 129, 131-135
Amir, Yigal 146
Amos 52, 56
anekantavada (non-one-sidedness) .71
Anti Defamation League 127
anti-Semitism 30, 122, 123
appreciation of difference 116
Aquinas, Thomas 35, 37
Arab - Israeli conflict 121, 122, 140
argument for the sake of heaven 69
Ariarajah, S. Wesley 91
Arizona Interfaith Movement, ... 32, 47
assimilation 121, 124
Augustine 35, 36
authentic religions 76
authenticity in prayer 104, 106
Ba'al Shem Tov, Israel 147, 153
Baha'i 20, 31, 47
Bar Kappara 52
Barrows, John Henry 20
Bauman, Zygmunt 82-83
Bayfield, Tony 90-91
Ben Azzai 436, 54, 57-59
bigotry 88, 132, 134, 145
Birkat Haminim 132-134
Bonney, Charles Carroll .. 20-21, 24, 25,
  26, 33, 40
Braybrooke, Marcus 31
bricolage 83-84, 112-114

Buber, Martin 13, 95-96, 158
Buddhism 17, 19, 23, 24, 39, 81, 96,
  114, 118
Cameron, William E. 19
capitalism 144
caricatures of religion 99
certainty as a human need 142
chosen people 103, 126, 145
Christian interpretive model 97
Christian superiority 20
Christianity ....
  Catholicism .. 23, 27-28, 44, 111, 113
  evangelical 28, 44
  liberal 17, 22
  Mennonite 31
  pre-millenialist 110
  Protestant 19, 20, 21, 29
  Western 20
circumcision 44, 56, 93
civil society 103
Cohen, Randy 116
colonialism 22, 29, 139, 144, 146
Columbian Exposition 15-21, 38, 80
common origin of humanity 59
communism 144
Confucianism 19, 33, 46, 47
contingency ... 23, 62, 63, 65, 67-68, 71,
  73, 83, 100, 156
Cook, Joseph 27, 28-29
Council for the Parliament of World
  Religions 40
creation in God's image 58, 115
creedal religion 81, 147
crucifix 112, 113, 114
Crypto-Jews 111-113
Crypto-Judaic identity 113
cultural and religious differences ... 116
  leading to misjudgement 102
cultural identity 102
cultural morality of the majority 115
cultural norms 117
cultural symbols 109
Dalai Lama 76
defining religion 80-81
denial of the other 126

169

Derrida, Jacques 83, 84
dialectic
    Hegelian 12, 61, 69, 97, 99
    open-ended 69-70, 97
    Talmudic 63, 70
    Talmudic and Jain 61, 73-74, 97
dialogue
    Buberian 94-96
    building understanding 89, 90
    conservative resistance 98-99
    content-less 94
    content-rich 95
    defining 90
    failure to examine challenging
        issues 91-92
    idiosyncratic and local 93-94
    imposition of self 94
    informal 90
    non-traditional voices 99
    objectification 94-95
    preconditions 94
    presence of atheists and agnostics
        99
    transformational 117
dialogue and debate 98-99
Dialogue with Trypho 13, 87
dichotomy
    primitive and civilized 18-19
dietary restrictions 117-119
diversity
    ecumenical verses interreligious 9
diversity of human religious
    expression 107
divinely sanctioned societal norm. 132
doctrines of relativity 71
Dodson, Charles 140-142
dominant/dominated dichotomy 80
Eckankar 106
Eidels, Samuel (Maharsha) 54
environment 32, 80, 91
essential messages
    of Reform Judaism 26-27
    of religion .. 21, 25, 26, 39, 41, 75, 80,
        92
    of Torah 52
essential unity of religion 23
ethic of reciprocity .... *See* golden rule
ethnocentrism 101
evolution
    Darwinian 17, 22, 80-81, 157
    natural selection 17
    social Darwinism (Spenserism) . 139
    social evolution 15-20, 22, 24, 27,
        80-81, 82
    social evolutionary tree 18
    Spencerian 17, 22
exclusive triumphalist model 144
exclusivist 27-28
false consciousness 102
family of religions 78
Geertz, Clifford 129
gender 9, 44, 83, 84, 92-94, 96, 106,
    109, 114, 130-131, 129, 150
gender equality 130-131
Gensler, Henry 42, 43, 44, 45
Gibbons, James Cardinal 27-28
Gilded Age 15, 17
Gillman, Neil 7, 100, 148
Gitlitz, David 113
Global Congress of World Religions . 31
global society 117, 139
globalism 139
globalization 9
Gmeiner, John 23
God of Abraham 78, 79, 122
golden rule 10, 11, 21, 33, 44, 38, 41,
    55, 73, 78, 80, 82, 83, 89, 91, 96, 97,
    105, 115, 116, 125, 139, 144, 146
    19th Century America 38
    a light commandment 60
    alternative reading 42
    basis of dialogue 45, 96
    brotherhoods 38
    Christian scripture 35
    Christian value 22, 23, 35, 46
    danger of misuse 41
    essence of revelation 36
    essential message of religion. 12, 36,
        46, 49
    expression of natural law 36
    imposed unity 49
    Jewish sources 51, 53-55, 56, 58

modern philosophical thought 38
negative formulation..................53-55
philosophic critiques..................36-38
potential danger in multi-faith context..44-45
role in 20th century 38
shared ethic...................................10
source of race hatred 30
source of unity 12
unifying ethic.................33, 34, 45
universal ethic...........................36-38
universality 34
universalizing message 46
weakness of negative formulation 55
world religions..........................46-48
golden rule day 38
golden rule movement 105
Goldstein, Baruch 146
good works 26
Gordis, Daniel 69
Gospel of John 16
Gospel of Matthew 34
great principle of the Torah.36, 51, 54, 57, 58, 60
great world religions................20, 29
development of concept 16, 20
Grim, John A. 80
Guide for the Perplexed 153
Guru Nanak 119
halakhah (Jewish Law)... 64, 68, 69, 70, 124
fundamental principle 65
nature of 69
halakhic process..............................68
Ha-Levi, Judah 13, 87
Hasidic theology............................154
Hasidism.147, 151, 154, 155, 156, 159
Hay, John 38
Hebrew Union College-Jewish Institute of Religion 9
Heschel, Abraham Joshua.............128
Higginson, Thomas Wentworth .24-25, 27, 77
Hillel 51, 53, 54, 55, 69, 73
Hillel, house of................................64

Hinduism........10, 17, 19, 23, 25, 30, 96, 118, 123
as monotheistic tradition..............123
Hirai, Ryuge Kinzo...........................29
Hirsch, Emil Gustav.........24, 25-27, 77
Hispanics........................ 17, 111, 112
hitlabbeshut (clothing itself in materiality) 154
Holiness Code............................ 53, 55
Holocaust 121
homocentric view of the world 17
Hordes, Stan 112
hunter-gatherer societies 18
Hunting of the Snark 140-141
I and Thou.......................................95
identity construction 43, 78, 83, 93
imitatio dei 56, 158
imposed hierarchy 48
incarnation 25
indigenous people 17, 80
indigenous religion................79, 80, 82
interfaith interaction 11, 13, 15, 20, 30, 31, 41, 42, 51, 61, 85, 89, 103, 104, 107, 121, 126, 146
interfaith movement 20, 21, 32, 47, 78, 85, 98, 103, 146
interfaith prayer services 104, 106, 125, 126
interreligious... usage 79
intra-faith relations 45, 89, 92, 165
Islam..10, 11, 18, 19, 24, 25, 27, 44, 78, 79, 87, 88, 93, 96, 99, 102, 105, 106, 114, 118, 121,144
Islamic nations................................18
Islamophobia.................................102
Jabara, Christopore 24
Jainism.5, 12, 19, 23, 24, 61, 62, 70-74, 97, 105, 114, 119, 152, 157
Jewish - Christian relations.............122
Jewish - Muslim dialogue 122
Jewish and Muslim relations 122
Jewish identity 111, 112, 113, 149
Jewish Theological Seminary of America............................. 7, 9, 151

171

Jewish, Christian and Muslim relations 79, 122
Jewish-Christian dialogue 13, 79, 87, 88, 90
joint prayer 104, 106, 107
jonglerie 84
Judaism
   Conservative 7, 9, 132, 151
   non-Orthodox as heritics 131
   Orthodox 99, 102, 115, 129, 151
   rabbinic 51
   Reconstructionist 128, 131
   Reform .9, 24, 26, 124, 131,133, 147, 150, 151
   traditional 62, 81, 102, 125, 130
   ultra-Orthodox 102
Justin 13, 36, 87
Kalam 87, 90
Kant, Immanuel 37, 38, 42
kashrut 43, 65, 117, 118, 143
Kishimoto, Nobuto 33, 39
klal gadol ...... *See* great principle of the Torah, *See* great principle of the Torah
klal yisrael 131
Küng, Hans 11, 14, 31, 32, 38, 39
Kunin, Seth 8, 84, 112
Kuzari 13, 87
legislation against traditional clothing 102
Levi-Strauss, Claude 83, 84
literal-golden rule fallacy 42
liturgy
   conservative aspect of religious life 126
living myth 100
Locke, John 37, 42
Lookstein, Haskel 125
Luria, Isaac (The Ari) 153, 155, 159
Lurianic mystical myth 155
Lyotard, Jean-Francois 82
Mahavira 72
manifest destiny 19, 157
Masuzawa, Tomoko 16, 20, 79, 81
mediums
   vehicles of communication 110

metaphor of a diamond 153
Midway 18, 19
minority opinions 67-68
missionaries 19, 21, 29
mitzvot 11, 53, 54, 70, 128, 130, 151
Moby Dick 45, 96
monotheism .. 11, 17, 19, 22, 26, 27, 81, 82, 89, 93, 106, 122, 123, 124, 145, 157
   ethical 11, 27
Mormon Church 17, 20, 118
multi-faith movement 16, 32, 105
Multi-Faith Saskatchewan 47
multiplicity of correct answers 67
multiplicity of differing paths 15
multiplicity of perspectives 70
multiplicity of truths 12, 62, 63, 64
mystical unity of religion 31
myth of Western superiority 16, 19
mythological thinking 84, 100
narrative ....
   acceptance of diversity 106, 107, 109, 127
   Christian unity 21
   conformity 88
   essential message .12, 21, 26, 27, 34, 38, 39, 40, 46, 47, 48, 52, 60, 61, 62, 73, 74, 75, 76, 79, 82, 83, 85, 92, 94, 96, 101, 104, 105, 125, 146
   exclusivity 11, 20, 21, 30
   foundational 16
   group identity 84
   inclusivity 11, 20, 21, 23, 30
   pluralism 11, 12, 20, 21, 29, 87
   religious essentialism 61, 65, 75, 77, 80, 83
   unity ... 11, 12, 19, 21, 25, 30, 34, 105
   unity of mission 11, 21, 30, 31
   unity, problematized 27
National Interfaith Conference on Peace 31
Native Americans 17, 18
native spirituality 47-48
natural law 25, 34, 36, 37, 38, 39
natural religion 25, 28

nayavada (perspectives) 71
Noachide laws 125, 144
North American Interfaith Network (NAIN) 40, 48
objectivity 101
objects of communication 110
obligations to the stranger 56
Origin of Species 17
overemphasis of similarities 88
Panikkar, Raimon 45, 96
Parliament of World Religions 24, 31, 38, 39, 40
participant observation 101, 103
particularism 144, 146
peace 9, 10, 11, 12, 30, 31, 32, 59, 75, 85, 89, 90, 91, 94, 126, 140, 144, 145, 147, 150
people of the book 78
Pittsburgh Platform 26
platinum rule 42
pluralism 11, 15, 20, 21, 126, 137
polytheistic religion 25, 78, 123
pon y seca 112-113, 154
positivist approach 99
post-modernism 7, 11, 61, 82
Potok, Chaim 150, 151
poverty 9, 10, 30, 75, 91
primitive nations 18
primitive religions 19, 82
process theology 22
progress theology 22
proselytization 29, 55, 83, 121
Protestant Christian triumphalism 15, 16
Qur'an 59, 106
race 17, 30, 44, 114-115
racism 15, 30
relativism
  Jain 71
  Western 72
religion
  as cause of hatred 132
  as source of intolerance and oppression 30, 137
  essential characteristic 22
Religious Workers for Lasting Peace 31
repetitive observance 128
retablos and *bulitos* 113
Robinson, Michael 150, 151
roles of women 94, 102
Rollins, Peter 94
Roth, Joel 7, 68, 69
Russell, Bertrand 37
Sacks, Jonathan 145
Schindler's List 59
secular belief systems 99
self-satisfaction of similarity 91
semiotic theory 18, 109, 113
Sermon on the Mount 34
sexism 102
sexual mores 102
sexuality 44, 102
Sforno, Obadiah ben Jacob 145
shamanism and fetishism 82
Shammai 53, 69, 74
Shammai, house of 64
Shaw, George Bernard 37, 42
Shintoism 19
Shneur Zalman of Liadi 153
Siddur Sim Shalom 131, 132, 169
Sikh *langur* (communal meal/soup kitchen) 119
Sikhism 10, 20, 30, 75, 151
Simlai, Rabbi 51
skepticism 72
social justice 10, 21, 30, 75, 151
soft-golden rule fallacy 42, 44
Soyen, Shaku 30
Sperber, Daniel 123
spiritual journeys 14, 147, 148, 152
spontaneous religious experiences 25
status of the Jewish people viv-a-vis other religions 131
status of woman within Orthodox Jewish life 129, 131
stereotypes 29, 43, 78, 91, 117, 128
swastika 13, 114
Swedenborgian Church 20
Swindler, Leonard 90, 94
syadvada (the maybe doctrine) 71
symbols

multiplicity of meanings 112
syncretism 21, 24, 25, 98, 99, 104
Taoism 19, 39
Temple of Understanding 31, 41
The Death of Death 100
The Dignity of Difference, ... 145
The Elephant and the Blind Men 71-73, 91, 153, 157
The Ethicist 115-116
the oven of Aknai 65
the Tower of Babel 145
theological reasoning 148
Tikkun Olam 197, 211
tolerance or mutual understanding 115, 180
Towards a Global Ethic 31, 38-39
traditional dress codes 130
transformation.... 12, 13, 14, 30, 43, 53, 61, 65, 85, 93, 97, 98, 105, 113, 148, 151
triumphalist prayers 127
Twain, Mark 143
tzimtzum (contraction) 155
ultimate truths 22, 29, 62
Unitarianism 225, 47
United Religions Initiative (URI) 40
United States
  mythic understanding 16
unity in diversity 23
universal culture 143, 144
  danger 143
universal kinship 58
universal model of society 83, 144
universal religion 25, 26, 28
universalism 139, 144, 145, 146
universality of religion 26
Vedanta movement 23
vegetarianism 73, 117, 118, 119
Vivekananda 23
War Prayer 143
Wattles, Jeffrey ... 33, 35, 36, 38, 40, 46, 47, 48, 105
Weatherhead, Leslie 147
Webb, Mohammed 27
weltanschauung 78, 84, 85
western capitalistic society 139
White City 18
Wicca 31, 47, 48, 49, 114, 152
Wiccan Rede 49, 152
Williams, Fannie Barrier 30
World Conference on Religion and Peace 31
World Congress of Faith 31, 40
World's Congress Auxiliary 20-21
World's Parliament of Religions 11, 15, 17, 19, 32, 33, 34, 39, 51, 75, 77, 82, 87, 90, 98, 101
worldview 19, 51, 60, 61, 72, 73, 82, 84, 94, 96, 103, 111, 112, 113, 127, 129, 156
xenophobia 88, 124
Yu, Pung Kwang 33
Zohar 155, 158
Zoroastrianism 19, 23, 24, 87, 114

Other Gaon Books
on Jewish History and Thought
and Comparative Religion

Gloria Abella Ballen. 2014. *The Power of the Hebrew Alphabet.* **Winner Best Book in Religion 2014.** New Mexico/Arizona Book Awards. Nominated Best Book, Jewish Book Awards, 2015.

Susana Weich-Shahak. 2014. *Moroccan Sephardic Romancero: An Anthology of an Oral Tradition.* **Winner of the European Folklore Prize, 2014. Finalist Best Book 2014,** New Mexico/Arizona Book Awards.

Ruth Sohn. 2013. *Crossing Cairo: A Jewish Woman's Encounter with Egypt.* **Finalist Best Book 2013, New Mexico/Arizona Book Awards. Jewish Book Council, Authors Network Selection.**

William Samelson. 2013. *Sephardic Legacy: Stories and Songs from Jewish Spain.*

Ron Duncan Hart. 2012. *Islam and Muslims: Religion, History and Ethnicity.* **Finalist, Best Book in Anthropology. 2012, New Mexico/Arizona Book Awards.**

Rafael David Elmaleh and George Ricketts. 2012. *Jews under Moroccan Skies: Two Thousand Years of Jewish Life.*

Rabbi Zalman Schachter-Shalomi and Netanel Miles-Yepez. 2011. *A Hidden Light: Stories and Teachings of Early HaBad and Bratzlav Hasidism.* **Winner, Best Book in Religion. 2012.** New Mexico/Arizona Book Awards.

Rabbi Zalman Schachter-Shalomi and Michael L. Kagan. 2011. *All Breathing Life Adores Your Name: The Interface between Prayer and Poetry.*

Rabbi Min Kantrowitz. 2010. *Counting the Omer: A Kabbalistic Meditation Guide.* **Finalist, Best Book in Religion. 2011.** New Mexico/Arizona Book Awards. "Book of Note", Jewish Book Council.

Gaon Books
in association with
Gaon Institute for Tolerance Studies
a 501-c-3 organization
Education about Jewish Life and Thought
www.gaoninstitute.org

CPSIA information can be obtained at www.ICGtesting.com
Printed in the USA
BVOW04s1940130415

395972BV00001B/9/P